# Campaign '08
## A Turning Point For Digital Media

Kate Kaye
With Foreword by Dan Solomon

# CONTENTS

# FOREWORD

2008 was a milestone year in political communications, and this book marks a milestone in its own right, as the first to delve deeply into the digital marketing efforts of the 2008 presidential campaigns. With the keen insights of an accomplished reporter, Kate Kaye pulls back the curtains to reveal what the campaigns tried and to what effect.

It is clear that digital communications made a difference in '08 – not just to the achievements of the Obama campaign, but for traditional political entities as well as news organizations and media outlets.

In fact, the year marked one milestone after another as we observed events and had experiences that were highly unlikely just a few short months earlier.

The Dow Jones Industrial Average lost almost 34 percent of its value.

Oil prices reached $147 a barrel, and gasoline prices averaged $4.11 per gallon nationwide. Then both plummeted.

During the 2008 Summer Olympics, Usain Bolt won an Olympic gold medal by running the 100-meter final in an astounding world record time of 9.69 seconds. His 19.30-second 200-meter, another world record, got him another gold.

Over half of adult Americans had broadband connections at home, and 96 percent of U.S. workers who connected to the Internet did so with broadband.

Nearly 2 percent of all U.S. homes received at least one foreclosure filing during the year.

In the first half of 2008, people downloaded millions of Apple iPhone and iTouch applications, and more than 10,000 applications were available by the end of the year.

Yet, arguably the year's greatest milestone was the election of the first African-American President of the United States, with 66,882,230 votes.

But isn't every Presidential election a milestone?  And perhaps the success of the campaigns in using digital techniques during 2008 was a result of the campaigns being in the right place at the right time. As Kate points out in her text, "In 2004, YouTube did not exist." And she reports that when it came to some elements of the campaigns, the full potential of digital communications was not embraced.

Kate reminds us that despite the wiz bang of new gadgets and digital platforms, communications is still a human endeavor. And like all human endeavors, cooperation and initiative make a difference in the outcome.

In this regard, one of my favorite vignettes from the book describes a consultant who handled search ads for the Democratic National Convention. The consultant was handed a detailed spreadsheet from the Obama campaign which identified search advertising terms to buy and others to avoid. As Kate suggests, the concept was a simple one. The national party did not want to compete with its own nominee's campaign for top search ad results.

This story is compelling because it demonstrates the benefits of teamwork in making digital techniques effective. Indeed, I believe that campaigns are successful, not because of the techniques they deploy, but because of their organization and purpose in deploying them.

In a sense, President Obama affirmed this belief during his Inaugural Address when he said, "Our challenges may be new. The instruments with which we meet them may be new. But those values upon which our success depends – hard work and honesty, courage and fair play, tolerance and curiosity, loyalty and patriotism – these things are old."

In Campaign '08: A Turning Point for Digital Media, we learn that the use of the Internet by the 2008 campaigns was evolutionary rather than revolutionary. In making this observation, no disparagement of any campaign or their talented teams is intended. To the contrary, the people behind the digital efforts of the 2008 presidential campaigns took advantage of their historical moment to a great degree. However, I believe the observation supports Kate's conclusion: We have not yet seen the pinnacle of the impact digital techniques will make.

Perhaps the greatest consequence of their efforts will be evidenced by future campaigns and their willingness to take advantage of the rapidly changing media environment in order to win.

Dan Solomon
CEO, Virilion

# ACKNOWLEDGMENTS

A few notes from the author:

Information and insights in this book were provided through a variety of research reports and sources. In addition to interviews conducted for articles published in ClickZ's Campaign '08 section throughout 2007 and 2008, I spoke with members of the inner circles of the McCain and Obama campaigns after the election to provide invaluable background. To ensure candor, I agreed to withhold their identities.

Many of the specifics on the online campaign ads primarily came from two sources: Nielsen Online and The Media Trust Company.

The following people deserve special thanks for their help with this book:

To my husband Steve, for eleven years of humoring my political rants and his constant support in all my endeavors.

To Michael Bassik, for helping me realize that online political advertising can be a real reporting beat.

To Read Scott Martin, for helping me keep ClickZ's Campaign '08 ad gallery stocked with presidential ads.

To Dan Solomon, for planting the book seed.

To the design and editorial teams at Virilion, for contributing their time and expertise to this book.

To Anna Maria Virzi and Zach Rodgers, for giving me the leeway to spend days inspecting Nielsen ad reports and Federal Election Commission filings for my ClickZ Campaign '08 stories.

To Corinna Chang and Michelle McGiboney of Nielsen Online, for providing invaluable reports on online political ads.

To Joe Murphy, for his longtime legal assistance and support.

Cheers,
Kate Kaye
January 2009
Jersey City, New Jersey

# CAMPAIGN '08: YEARS IN THE MAKING

What a difference eight years make.

In the 2008 election, John McCain was mocked as the old man who didn't understand technology. His campaign obviously didn't *get* the Web, observers said.

By contrast, these political trackers said, Barack Obama's campaign was with it. They ran in-game ads and told supporters about the choice of Joe Biden as Obama's running mate via text messages. They *got* digital media.

It was pretty easy for onlookers to define the two presidential campaigns the way they defined the candidates themselves. McCain was the wrinkly guy who could barely check his e-mail. Obama was the younger, fresher, innovative man of change. Surely their campaign operations could be categorized in the same manner, right? Not exactly.

McCain was separated from a Web-savvy reputation by one Bush administration. He and his Web team had been praised in 2000 by politicos for taking a forward-thinking, Internet-driven approach to organizing, building support, and generating online donations. The Arizona senator's Republican primary campaign put the Web on the political map. Suddenly, the notion of a Web site being a central campaign hub and fundraising machine made sense. Using e-mail to rally local supporters had helped him give

George W. Bush a run for his money in the early primaries.

McCain lost that race, of course.

It would take another failed primary effort to make people really notice the Internet and its ability to alter political campaigning. In the '04 Democratic presidential primaries Howard Dean's campaign manager, Joe Trippi, became a darling of the burgeoning online political scene. He took e-mail and online fundraising to another level, and cool digital tools like Meetup helped foster a community of Dean supporters that could have never existed if it weren't for the Internet. But Dean lost his primary bid.

In 2008, the early adopters were back. Trippi ran the Web team for Democrat John Edwards. Some of the same folks who helped the McCain campaign online in 2000 (and George Bush's re-election effort in '04) were with McCain for another go-round. Some of the people who ran the e-campaign for Bush/Cheney '04 were with Mitt Romney, and others were with Fred Thompson. Some Kerry Web people went on to help Hillary Clinton's digital marketing team.

They all lost, too (except for some of the Clinton Web folks who went on to work for Obama's campaign).

The point is as much as the 2008 strategies will inform campaigns for years to come, they owe a debt to campaigns that had gone before. It took a lot of people and a lot of trial and a lot of error to get to 2008, the election season when even mainstream newspapers took note of Internet campaigning. It was the election that had digital media firms coming out of the woodwork to try to score political ad dollars. It was the election when everything digital seemed to come together: the community building, the organizing tools, the video, the social networking, the blogger engagement, the e-mail, the text messaging, and yes, the advertising.

But neither of the two main presidential campaigns can be used as a template for the next time around. For one thing, digital media moves way too fast. Just think: Search advertising was barely a consideration for the '04 campaigns, and YouTube didn't even exist!

Today when people hear the words "election" and "Internet," they think "Obama." But was it really his campaign's Internet strategy that enabled his win? Surely it fueled momentum among supporters, enabled unparalleled organizing efforts, and brought in tons of cash – enough so that he could ignore public funding and the limitations that go with it.

But the momentum and fundraising ability wouldn't have been there if he'd been just any old candidate. Dean and McCain 2000 couldn't get past the primaries despite their Web innovations. McCain's 2008 campaign was far more advanced in terms of digital strategy than previous Republican and Democratic campaigns, yet we know what happened there. Ron Paul built up a significant online following in the 2008 Republican primaries but couldn't get past the cult candidate stage.

Obama was the right guy at the right time. Not only did he have the charisma and popularity, he was on the right...er...correct side of the aisle when it came to the maligned Bush presidency. McCain did not have those advantages. Obama had lots of other factors going for him, too, the dismal economy being a big one. McCain suffered from lackluster support among the Republican base and inadequate campaign funds.

Still, there's no question that the Internet strategy was a major component of Obama's campaign. There were, some say, 95 staffers dedicated to it!

Almost a hundred people were on staff for Obama just to run the Web show. Compare that to roughly 14 for the McCain campaign. About that many of Obama's staffers focused on digital marketing and advertising alone.

"I can't imagine a Republican campaign having 95 people working on their Internet team...and maybe that's simply a matter of resources," said Mike Turk, a tech consultant for Republicans who worked as Internet advisor for Thompson's campaign and served as e-campaign director for Bush/Cheney '04. In 2004, the Bush e-campaign team consisted of seven full time staffers, according to Turk.

And while all those Obama people were paid campaign staffers, McCain's small team included non-staffers from consulting firms and interns. People talked about that, about integration. How important did the McCain campaign people think the digital marketing or the Web in general should be? The conclusion: Not enough to consider it much more than an ATM. The Web team was charged with making money to help add a few coals to what sometimes seemed like fading embers. Limited staff and limited resources, coupled with a bootstrapped campaign, meant the Web would be used for fundraising and little else.

The online ad strategy was "not necessarily on message with the McCain campaign…it was as if Internet advertising existed as a separate silo within the campaign," said one observer. "It was as if they didn't care as long as the ads made money."

McCain's Internet team had to come home with a certain amount of money in their pockets every day. Groundbreaking utilization of the Internet – such as the VP text announcement – seemed to the McCain campaign too much like playing around and not enough like business.

The candidate was mocked as an out-of-touch rich guy for having 12 houses. Meanwhile, his campaign had to resort to the online ad equivalent of food stamps. Money was so tight at one point late in the primary season that the Web team arranged to pay publishers a portion of the donations they'd raised through display ads on their sites. Even when advertisers buy ads on a cost-per-click model, they pay a fee to the publisher. In this case, said a McCain Web team insider, "Nobody was being paid anything unless money was being raised." It was the first election cycle they'd tried the "revenue share" model.

Obama's digital people had directives, too: X cost for e-mail or advertising should garner X amount of money in donations or X number of signups. However, the Obama campaign had the money, people and resources to be more expansive: engage with its Facebook community or send e-mails that didn't beg for money every time.

The Obama Web team worked closely with campaign people handling other media efforts. For instance, when a direct mail piece focusing on a particular issue was planned to go out, they devised an online campaign in coordination. When TV ad people planned to film a new spot, they would ask the digital media team if they'd like anything filmed for online video purposes. Some online ad people were on the same e-mail list as the television ad staff. Late in the election season when the Obama camp used online advertising to promote voter registration and get out the vote efforts to younger people, the digital ad staff worked regularly with other media teams. And sometimes messaging developed by staffers handling digital media influenced messaging and images used for television and radio.

"We had the same creative….We wanted everything to come out as one voice," said an Obama Web staffer.

To some it seemed that McCain's Web operation was separate from the main campaign. The Web people didn't always get enough lead time when it came to messaging -- what issues the campaign planned to focus on in the coming weeks and how those issues would be communicated. Polling data that could have assisted in ad targeting decisions didn't always trickle down to the online ad people.

Major staff switch-ups in the summer of '07 didn't help. Flubs like running a "McCain Wins Debate!" ad online before the September 26 presidential debate actually occurred appeared amateurish.

While McCain's digital campaign people sometimes were disconnected and underappreciated, Obama's Web team was loved. The media clamored to know what they were doing to get so many Facebook friends and foster celebrity-laden YouTube videos. The rest of the campaign recognized that the Internet served as a focal point, not only for Facebook friends and fundraising, but organizing and get-out-the-vote efforts.

"The higher ups got this more than anybody else," said an online media exec who worked closely with the Obama campaign during the primaries. And because they recognized the Internet as so "incredibly important" for organizing and maintaining relationships with grassroots supporters, "they said, 'Let's use this for other things.' "

That integrated strategy paid off. While it wasn't the major factor in Obama's victory, it contributed significantly to his well-orchestrated election campaign, and helped mold the candidate's image as a competent, modern leader in a time of turmoil.

It's important to stress that McCain's Web people were savvy in their own right. But they were hampered because they weren't part of the inner circle. Obama's Web team, meanwhile, got to sit at the big kids' table.

# ABOUT THIS BOOK

If most media outlets covering the presidential campaigns had anything to say about it, Facebook, YouTube, blogs, and other social media phenomena would get all the credit for making 2008 the most digital election ever.

But that's only half the Web story. Surely no campaign staffer worth his salt would deny the potential impact of a Barack Obama supporter posting a link on her Facebook page to the candidate's site. However, the fact is many of the campaigns used a far more measurable online campaign tactic: paid online advertising.

Throughout the election season, the author of this book closely followed the paid efforts of the campaigns, observing their display and search advertising, how they bought online media, where they targeted their ads, what the goals were, and how much they spent. For this book the author spoke with people who were closely involved with the online presidential campaigns, including some from the McCain and Obama camps.

While it's clear that political advertisers are far behind commercial advertisers when it comes to adopting online advertising and devoting dollars to it, the '08 presidential campaigns were by far the most advanced political digital marketers in history.

As Democratic online ad evangelist and Air America Chief Digital Officer Michael Bassik put it, "I think that [Howard] Dean showed campaigns they needed to have a Web site, and it needed to be used for fundraising. [John] Kerry showed that e-mail is a great tool.... Obama showed you need a site, you need a big e-mail list, but you can also create a community. The Internet does not exist as a silo. It is the hub of the campaign."

As early as January 2007, candidates still in the exploratory stages had begun buying ad space on the Web. Granted, they spent little compared to what they allocated to television ads or even to Web site building and management. Still, Web ads enabled them to drive potential supporters to their sites in the hopes of getting them to sign up for e-mails, attend a house party, volunteer, or donate a few bucks.

Not only were display and search ads relatively inexpensive; because online ad results are measurable, they allowed the campaigns to determine whether their dollars were well spent before voters went to the polls.

Obama's campaign quickly came to symbolize Internet campaigning. But the fact is John McCain's campaign and others used Web advertising. Republican hopeful Mitt Romney hired seasoned interactive ad staff to run an especially innovative online effort. Republicans Tom Tancredo, Fred Thompson, and Mike Huckabee dabbled in online advertising along with Democrats Bill Richardson and John Edwards. Obama's Democratic primary rival Hillary Clinton also used Web ads to a limited degree.

The Democratic and Republican National Committees and other party organizations entered the fray on behalf of their candidates. Meanwhile, political action committees, advocacy groups, and 527s engaged in election-related digital marketing.

Election ads showed up across the Web. The likely suspects like CNN.com, Politico, and HuffingtonPost.com saw some political ad dollars, but Google was the biggest winner of campaign cash. Yahoo, Facebook, and local news sites also scored. Even the lesser known sites -- the long tail sites -- managed to reap the rewards through targeting of niche and local audiences via ad networks.

Ad creative ran the gamut from goofy to sober and positive to malicious. Campaigns used issues such as pork-barrel spending, immigration, gas prices, and the Iraq War to get the attention of Web users. They asked voters to sign online petitions, register to vote, and of course, donate.

Indeed, more than any other purpose, the campaigns used online advertising and other digital marketing efforts for fundraising. When the mainstream media acknowledged the importance of the Internet in community-building and fundraising, they got it right. What they failed to recognize was the role online advertising played.

# WHY THE PRESIDENTIAL CAMPAIGNS USED DIGITAL MARKETING

Fundraising, fundraising, fundraising. It's the main reason political campaigns advertise on the Web.

Ever since the McCain 2000 and Dean 2004 campaigns showed them the fundraising light, savvy political campaigns from president to city council have gotten serious about generating donations. No longer do they simply rely on viral marketing efforts to build supporter lists. In addition to using social tools and engaging communities on social networking sites, candidates' Web ads are almost entirely geared towards getting people to click-through and donate or provide contact information.

More people are comfortable with donating campaign cash online. The Pew Research Center reported in June 2008 that 8 percent of Internet users had donated money to a candidate online. In the fall of '06, just 3 percent said the same.

Early in the primary season, Obama and McCain sought to build their supporter lists, the goal being to return to them throughout the election via e-mail, asking for donations. The ubiquitous "Join Us" refrain used in Obama's display and search ads invited people to "help" the candidate or sign up to attend campaign events. That acted as the main ad-driven mechanism for intercepting contact information.

Clinton took a much more direct approach to fundraising: She asked straight out. On the heels of her big primary wins in Texas and Ohio, her campaign hoped to milk the momentum for all it was worth – even if it was just 5 or 50 bucks. Web ads on news sites urged supporters to "Contribute $50 Now." Meanwhile, e-mails sent by the campaign low-balled requests, asking people to give a mere $5.

"Web advertising is proven to be effective for fundraising. It largely depends on how it's targeted and where it's targeted," Mike Turk of the Thompson campaign said in March 2008. It makes sense for campaigns to target ads to geographic areas "where they have more strength or more supporters," he added.

Like most e-mails sent by political campaigns, messages from the Clinton campaign sent before the important Pennsylvania primary also begged for cash. One message claimed over 45,000 people contributed to the campaign after Clinton's Ohio and Texas primary wins. The goal was to raise $3 million in 24 hours, but the e-mail hit up supporters for just $5. "Give Hillary a head start with a $5 contribution today."

The Clinton ad effort bore a striking similarity to one from John Kerry's 2004 Democratic presidential campaign. His ads asked people to contribute specific amounts such as $25 or $50. Mitt Romney's campaign took a similar tack in Web ads that suggested supporters "Donate $44 for the Future 44th President."

One possible reason for the small donation tactic: donors of lower amounts could be tapped again and again before they reached the $2,300 threshold for contributions from individuals to candidates during the primary season. With every donation, a voter becomes more invested in a candidate and more likely to volunteer time, contribute more money and, most important, vote on election day.

About a year before, the Clinton campaign used display ads to get contact information. One ad invited people to "Sign the Petition" to end President Bush's veto threat against Iraq War-related legislation. A softer "Join the Conversation" call-to-action led to a page prompting users to register and learn more about her campaign.

The campaign also used search to build the supporter list, but Google's political ad man Peter Greenberger believed efforts were hampered by a failure to use advertising consistently throughout the primaries. "They had experimented with it early on in the campaign season, and then they ended up cutting it off the last two quarters of 2007," he said in June after Clinton dropped out of the race. By the time the campaign re-launched search ad efforts during the primaries, he believed, "they had already dug themselves into a huge hole in terms of how many small donors they could count on."

Continued Greenberger, "All along, the Obama campaign had been building this huge list, and Clinton wasn't even in the game."

Starting early would have prevented donor fatigue, he said. "The Clinton campaign was in the position of having to go back to donors very soon after they signed up," he explained, adding, "In general you hope that you're not in the process of building [a list] and using it at the same time. You don't want to burn through that list. The Obama campaign and the McCain campaign both understood this."

The McCain camp understood it as far back as January 2007, when it was still an exploratory committee running video ads that let supporters submit e-mail addresses and other contact info within the ads themselves. "It's all about the ROI," Eric Frenchman, chief Internet strategist at political consulting agency Connell Donatelli Inc., and the man behind the McCain camp's search advertising said at the time. He was referring to the holy grail for all advertisers, return on investment. "Obviously we're getting branding and messaging out there at the same time," he added.

McCain's campaign liked surveys and petitions from the start. Not only did they get people to register their contact information, they attached the candidate to issues that were central to his campaign. "$74 million tax dollars for peanut storage costs? That's Nuts!"

read ads seen throughout the election season. "Outraged by Pork? Sign the Petition."

As the economy worsened in 2008, McCain's Web campaign focused more and more on high gas prices. Ads asking if voters were "being robbed at the pump" prompted them to "Take the Survey." McCain ads also asked Web users to "Join John McCain," "Support John McCain," "Learn More," "Click Here," or "Play Video." The ultimate goal for most of them was to spur donations and build that list.

By September 2008, however, McCain was desperate to raise cash. His campaign took a more direct approach, following the Clinton school of online advertising. Up against Obama's powerful fundraising machine and campaign finance laws, the co-author of the McCain-Feingold campaign finance reform law established the McCain-Palin Compliance Fund to continue soliciting donations. Ads urged supporters to "Donate $50" to "Invest in Victory."

Though the candidates' Web ads were designed almost entirely with some direct call-to-action in mind, a few ad efforts attempted to persuade voters. Keep in mind many political consultants don't think Internet ads can be used to sway voters. Attempts to persuade voters through online advertising in 2008 may not convince them otherwise, but they did signal a willingness to consider Web ads as more than just a fundraising vehicle.

Ads with embedded video were the most obvious forms of persuasive display advertising. The Romney campaign was among the earliest to attempt persuasion through video and even standard display ads. In October 2007 – just in time for a FOX News debate among GOP hopefuls and a Values Voter Summit hosted by pro-marriage and family group Family Research Council – Romney spots on the TV airwaves in Iowa made their way into online ad units in video content. Viewers could click to watch the ad while pausing the video content clip.

But on those rare occasions that online ads are used to persuade, there's almost always a secondary or complementary goal. In the case of the Romney video ads, it was to collect contact info on the MittRomney.com registration page.

Obama's video ads seen before the Texas and Ohio primaries were used to persuade and gather signups. In addition to suggesting voters "Find your early-vote location," the TV spots embedded in the ads mentioned issues like healthcare, the war in Iraq and middleclass tax cuts to act as persuasion tools.

"They used the Web to get more exposure to the television ad," said an online media executive familiar with the effort.

Before the contentious Pennsylvania primary, the Obama camp hoped to convince voters that Clinton was beholden to oil and gas corporation lobbyists. This time, the campaign used non-video ads. "Hillary Clinton has taken more money from PACs and Washington lobbyists, including those for oil and gas, than anyone in the race," read the ads, which ran on Pennsylvania sites.

Romney's ads seen in early 2008 also aimed to persuade. "Republicans Have to Get Our Own House in Order. Stop wasteful spending. Secure the borders. Insist on high ethical standards," said some.

Certainly, some McCain ads seen throughout the election season could also be described as persuasive in their attempts to paint the Arizona senator as a strong, experienced leader. "One Man Has the Experience, One Man Has the Courage, One Man Has Our Trust," read some ads. They, too, served a dual purpose in their mission to get supporters to join the team.

Anti-Obama display ads were also persuasive in nature. "Foreign Policy? Taxes? National Security?" questioned one featuring a photo of the Democratic candidate. The ad concluded that Obama was "Not Ready To Lead."

It wasn't until the final weeks of the election season that McCain and Obama used Web ads to persuade voters in a more full-fledged manner. In fact, by October, the McCain campaign used the small number of display ads it was still running only for persuasion purposes.

Rather than simply targeting "Join Us" and fundraising ads to women, for instance, both camps showed them ads with actual messages intended to sway them. Voting for McCain/Palin was a vote for women's suffrage, a vote for female empowerment. Voting for Obama was a vote for women's reproductive rights. The two sparred on which campaign would stand up for equal pay for women.

Obama hoped to convince Jewish voters and other staunch supporters of Israel that he would defend that nation's security.

But the most crucial issue for most voters was the economy, and both camps focused on their tax plans to convince Americans that their economic ideas were best for the middle class. The Obama campaign pushed its "Tax Calculator" in Web ads in order to explain in a tangible way what the Obama tax plan would mean for them. And, as in his offline campaign, McCain used Joe the Plumber to represent his economic platform as the better one for everyday Americans and small businesses. His campaign even used imagery and colors seen in Obama's ads for months and suggested Obama had been lying about his voting record on taxes. "Come On Senator, Tell the Truth," said the ads.

Before election day, many wondered whether Obama's massive online community-building effort would translate into actual votes. If anything, the campaign made sure its Web ad strategy facilitated its get-out-the-vote goals. Before important primaries and before the November election, the campaign used Web ads to promote early voting, voter registration, and GOTV on election day. Ads placed on local sites before the Texas and Ohio primaries, along with the millions that were targeted to North Carolina primary voters, all aimed to get voters to the polls early.

As the general election neared, however, voter registration was of the utmost importance to Democrats (recognizing that newly registered voters are often younger, or immigrants who tend to favor Democrats).

Starting in the summer of '08, Obama's camp began running ads featuring a voter registration message. Ads seen in September were targeted to residents of specific states, reminding them of the last day they could register. "Register to Vote for Barack Obama and Other Candidates For Change," they said. An ad aimed at Pennsylvania voters noted, "To Vote In Pennsylvania You Need To Be Registered By October 6."

In addition, the Obama camp was bolstered by the Democratic National Committee, which led the online voter registration drive, running ads in English and Spanish to promote online voter registration.

The Obama campaign drew mainstream attention to a surprising late-season effort reminding voters that "Early Voting Has Begun." Ads aimed at online gamers in 10 battleground states were seen in a variety of games including EA's driving game, "Burnout Paradise," and "NBA Live 08."

VoteForChange.com ads promoting early voting flooded states that allowed people to vote before November 4 (though it appeared as though Florida residents saw the most of those). Even Americans living in other countries saw Obama's ads urging them to "Vote from Abroad." Then, when early voting ended, battleground state residents were hit with ads telling them "Find out where to vote" on the 4th.

Did the GOTV push work? It depends how you look at it.

Whether the extensive online GOTV efforts of the Obama campaign and Democratic Party had a significant impact on voter turnout will likely be debated for years to come. A few weeks after the election, a report from the American University

Center for the Study of the American Electorate suggested maybe they hadn't, at least when it came to the number of people who voted. However, Democratic voters came out in droves.

"Despite lofty predictions by some academics, pundits, and practitioners that voter turnout would reach levels not seen since the turn of the last century, the percentage of eligible citizens casting ballots in the 2008 presidential election stayed at virtually the same relatively high level as it reached in the polarized election of 2004," stated the November 6 report.

Projecting the final vote tally, the report estimated 126.5 million to 128.5 million eligible voters pulled levers in 2008. "If this prediction proves accurate, turnout would be at either exactly the same level as in 2004 or, at most, one percentage point higher."

Quoted in the report, CSAE director Curtis Gans said, "Many people were fooled (including this student of politics although less so than many others) by this year's increase in registration (more than 10 million added to the rolls), citizens' willingness to stand for hours even in inclement weather to vote early, the likely rise in youth and African American voting, and the extensive grassroots organizing network of the Obama campaign into believing that turnout would be substantially higher than in 2004…. But we failed to realize that the registration increase was driven by Democratic and independent registration and that the long lines at the polls were mostly populated by Democrats."

# THE MONEY

Was 2008 really the first true Internet election? The Internet itself, symbolized by the success of Barack Obama's campaign, has gotten kudos for helping him win the election. And there's little doubt that digital media had a significant effect on the victor's campaign. However, even though Obama for America was more dedicated to digital than any other campaign before it, the fact is the amount of money spent online does not reflect that.

Obama grabbed millions of dollars through online fundraising from countless donors giving relatively small amounts of cash. But, as in every election in recent history, the bulk of that money was spent on television ads.

And no matter how much John McCain's campaign finance reform efforts strived to curtail the influence of money on our democratic process, we can't realistically separate politics from money or money from politics.

If the 2008 election and Obama's campaign – the most expensive in history – truly were about change, why was the ad budget so biased toward traditional media? Try this for a comparison:

In October, The Wall Street Journal's Laura Meckler, citing Campaign Media Analysis Group, reported that the Obama camp had plunked down $3.3 million on TV spots in a single day. By comparison, the campaign spent less than that on Web media

– about $2.98 million – between January and April. It spent more for TV ads on a single mid-October Monday then it spent in four months online!

Obama's campaign spent more than $16 million on Web advertising in 2008, according to Federal Election Commission) reports. That's just 6 percent of the $250 million TNS Media Intelligence/ Campaign Media Analysis Group projected that Obama spent on television spots. Throw in the money spent on direct mail ads, telemarketing, radio and other ad efforts, and online seems more like a rounding error than an expenditure.

McCain's campaign spent far less. According to McCain's FEC reports, around $3.6 million was spent on Web media. Once all the numbers are in, that total may grow; however, it most likely won't reach even half of Obama's online ad spending.

These numbers do not include spending by either the Republican or Democratic National Committees on behalf of their candidates.

A precise comparison between the two campaigns is not possible. The McCain campaign's reports filed with the commission were quite cryptic, especially in comparison to Obama's. While Obama's included individual payments made to particular online media companies (GOOGLE INC., 07/26/2008, On-line Advertising, $3022.65), McCain's showed disbursements made to media consulting firms. It was known that expenditures for "media" made to Web ad consulting firm Connell Donatelli were payments for online ads. But making their reports even more opaque, the McCain camp listed Connell Donatelli as "CD, Inc." in its FEC filings.

## Top Recipients of Obama Campaign
## Online Media Spending

| Media Company | 2008 Estimated Total Paid |
| --- | --- |
| Google | $7,500,000 |
| Yahoo | $1,500,000 |
| Centro | $1,300,000 |
| Advertising.com | $947,000 |
| Facebook | $643,000 |
| CNN | $461,000 |
| Microsoft | $405,000 |
| AOL | $313,000 |
| Pulse 360 | $222,000 |
| Quigo | $195,000 |
| Collective Media | $168,000 |
| Politico | $151,000 |
| Blogads | $149,000 |
| Time | $147,000 |
| BET Digital | $138,000 |
| Pontiflex | $137,000 |
| Washington Post | $125,000 |
| Undertone Networks | $110,000 |
| The Weather Channel | $108,000 |
| Cox Communications | $100,000 |

Spending estimates compiled by the author from
Federal Election Commission reports.

It's debatable whether Web ads will ever make or break a campaign. Romney's e-strategy director, Mindy Finn, said Web ads can only go so far when it comes to building momentum for political campaigns. "While advertising is a fire starter, potentially, or a complementary method of getting a message out, it is never going to be as successful as a real grassroots ground-up type of movement," she said.

Online ads do not a movement make. But do campaigns put themselves at a disadvantage if they don't use paid online efforts in conjunction with the free or inexpensive tactics such as posting videos to YouTube or creating Facebook groups?

Consider Hillary Clinton's campaign. The contrast between Obama's online ad spending and that of Clinton's had some wondering whether more of her ad budget should have been spent online( Her FEC filings show that only around $500,000 went to online ads.)

Indeed, a source familiar with Clinton's online campaign said there also wasn't much of a budget carved out for online display ads. It's a tale often told by digital marketers in the commercial world: The people behind some of Clinton's Web advertising say they had to practically beg for scraps of cash. Five grand here, 10K there. The digital media buyers would immediately throw the money towards fundraising ads, often bought on news sites like CNN.com.

Frequently the response was rewarding. A $5,000 media buy would turn into $15,000 in donations. But despite the scattered success, some Web ads never got a dedicated share of the Clinton media budget.

Every four years, online politicos cling to the notion that THIS will be the election year, the one that moves a significant amount of money away from TV toward the Internet. Yet, though both the Obama and McCain campaigns spent more money and resources on Web efforts and ads than in any past presidential election,

2008 symbolized more of a stimulus for a major shift in media budget allocation than actually representing a major shift.

Analysts' expectations for how much political advertisers would spend in 2008 ranged from about $20 million to $110 million, or between 1 percent and 4 percent of what they predicted for political ad spending across all media. The forecasts varied because methodologies varied from research firm to research firm.

But the takeaway was the same. Be it 1 percent or 4 percent, it seems like a blip on the screen. Consider this: Online advertising accounts for 8.7 percent of all U.S. ad revenues across all media, according to an August eMarketer report. Needless to say, political advertisers trail behind commercial advertisers when it comes to the amount of money they allocate to digital advertising and marketing efforts.

"I was very surprised to see how little was spent," said Bassik. "Across the board there's been more growth in online ad spending than any other medium from corporations…. The reverse still holds true for political."

Kip Cassino, (vice president of research for Borrell Associates, one of the research firms) that predicted online political ad spending, said in October that he expected the 2008 election would inspire future campaigns to boost online ad spending. "What we'll find is the Senate and gubernatorial campaigns... are going to start to spend as much as the presidential campaigns did this year," he said.

And, in turn, local campaigns will graduate to bigger online ad budgets as well. "They'll move up to what the regional and statewide campaigns did this cycle," Cassino added.

There are lots of reasons why political campaigns don't spend more on the Web:

1. Political media consultants are conditioned to buying TV.

*VoTE iQ needs to hire a RESOURCE that works with media consultants so they understand how to optimize & on the sine. — (via media consultant)*

*VoTE iQ Media SPECIALISTS — 1*

2. They don't understand how to buy or target online ads.

3. They don't think their audience is online.

4. Wed ads are relatively inexpensive.

5. They don't believe online advertising can be used for persuasion.

6. They make far more commissions on TV ads than they do when buying Web ads.

7. And that's not all.

Habit is a major deterrent preventing people from trying any new technology, and media consultants are creatures of habit, too. They're used to buying TV and radio ads. They're conditioned to buying direct mail and newspaper ads. Buying Internet advertising remains a mystery for many political media buyers. Though there are countless evangelists trying to woo them toward the Internet, many ad buyers are not aware of what online advertising and marketing offers.

According to a study conducted in July 2007 for E-Voter Institute, more than 70 percent of political consultants have hesitations about using digital media. "Really, the underlying issue is they just don't know how to buy (online)," E-Voter Institute President Karen Jagoda said in 2007. Considering the tight time parameters political consultants maneuver in, many simply do what they know – or think – works, rather than trying something new.

Some also don't realize the unique audience targeting capabilities the Web affords. The E-Voter Institute report noted that many political consultants believe their campaigns can't target accurately online. The reality is quite different. While TV and radio ads result in a great deal of waste for political campaigns that sometimes need only to reach a specific region, online advertising can be targeted down to the ZIP code. Combine that with the ability to reach specific demographic groups in specific types of content, and the targeting capability far exceeds traditional media.

Misconceptions about the online population also exist. The common belief is digital media platforms are great places to reach Democrats and liberals. Therefore, the thinking goes, traditional media – TV, direct mail, telephone, newspaper, and radio – are the best places to target right-wingers. The E-Voter Institute report reflects this way of thinking. Around 75 percent of consultants said blogs, podcasts, e-mail, and candidate Web sites are effective for communicating with liberal activists. About 65 percent said online ads and social sites are effective.

Meanwhile, at least 70 percent of the political consultants polled said TV, cable and radio ads, direct mail, and debates are effective for getting the attention of conservatives. Online ads were deemed effective for reaching those on the right by just 51 percent.

There's also the simple fact that online advertising is relatively inexpensive. This is especially true of the direct-response oriented stuff political campaigns tend to buy. For many types of online ads, they only have to pay when someone clicks on them or takes a certain action. Though it's an attractive proposition for advertisers, it also means many of the ads we see on the Web are a cheap commodity.

"I don't think there's room for online advertising to have a much greater share," Romney for President's Finn said in January 2008, referring to the campaign's ad budget. "One thing to remember is that online advertising is just so much cheaper," she added. Still, she acknowledged that more money could be spent on ad creative or other online initiatives.

"It's definitely less expensive," said Bassik. But, he continued, there's a special element about a political campaign that most commercial brand advertisers can only dream about. People – through blogs, e-mail, video uploads, and other social media – are out there on the Web carrying that virtual banner promoting their candidate early on, sometimes long before campaigns are even made official.

For example, if "GE needs to invest in social media assistance;

they need advertising," he said. Political campaigns – particularly campaigns centered around a charismatic candidate such as Obama – he argued, don't necessarily need to advertise as much online. Supporters, in essence, do it for them. "That said, it was completely lopsided for both campaigns…a missed opportunity to reach and persuade voters online."

Another important factor is that political consultants typically don't believe Internet ads can be used to sway voters. Like the old belief among commercial advertisers that the Web can't be used for branding purposes, most in the political world see Internet advertising as a direct-response medium. Web ads can be used to collect e-mail addresses and donations, but they don't have the emotive or persuasive power of television, they say. When it comes to the Web, political advertisers rely on things like video on YouTube and their official sites to have persuasive impact.

Then there are the commissions. Once other reasons are exhausted, oftentimes the dirty little secret of media consulting comes out: Consultants make higher commissions from buying pricier television ads than they do when buying Web ads. Unless the candidate or campaign management is begging for online ads, why not throw most if not all the ad budget to traditional media where the pay is a lot better?

But wait! All that will change after 2008, right? Surely, if McCain's and Dean's primary campaigns' online fundraising successes didn't convince them to learn about the Web, Obama's groundbreaking efforts certainly should.

"This was the watershed event," said Jeff Dittus, founder and CEO of Campaign Grid, a consulting and technology firm that ran online efforts for 10 Republican Senate campaigns and eight Republican House campaigns in 2008. Dittus believes by the mid-term elections of 2010, lots of money will move online from budgets currently allocated to things like direct mail.

Yet, if political campaigns recognize the Web's value and allocate more resources there, that does not necessitate a huge influx of money will move toward online ads or marketing efforts in the near future.

Campaigns take advantage of as much free online media as possible. YouTube, social media interaction, Facebook and MySpace profiles, search engine optimization, user-generated video, and other digital platforms cost little if nothing to utilize.

"Candidates are spending tremendous amounts of resources, time, and energy to use the Internet, but in terms of paid political advertising, the lower estimates are more likely," Bassik said.

Also, campaigns are so concerned with keeping up when it comes to TV spending, the Web often gets put on the backburner.

So, although there are reasons why more political money isn't moving to the Internet, there is growth, and mindsets are changing. Said E-Voter's Jagoda, "We're getting to the point where enough money is being spent that we can start asking questions about line items in the budget."

# ABOUT THE ADS

If there's one thing that separated Obama's ads from McCain's, it was the consistent imagery. Practically all of Obama's display ads (often called banner, image, or graphical ads) featured the candidate's smiling image. In millions of ads, his campaign logo rose like the sun on the horizon and sometimes showed his ubiquitous "The Change We Need" message, almost always introducing Obama's face against a signature azure blue backdrop. Reflecting the general tack of the entire campaign, the message was a simple, positive one: "Join Us."

"If you had to say one thing about Obama's ad creative, it was consistency," said one Democratic consultant, noting that the display ad colors, imagery, and language matched the vision, rhetoric, and aesthetic that was carried through in other media. "The mail looked like the ads, looked like the site, the TV ads, the Web banners, the T-shirts….There was consistency to the branding that reinforced his offline or overarching message."

In contrast, many of McCain's display ads – and, like Obama's, there were millions upon millions served up across the Web – didn't even mention his name, much less show his face. Instead, Web users were greeted with images of a young couple poring over bills at a kitchen table, a gas station sign showing too-high fuel prices, even a grizzly bear, and photos of Paris Hilton and Fidel Castro.

But before McCain and Obama emerged as the top contenders in the '08 race, several Democratic and Republican presidential contenders ran ads ranging from the hopeful to hateful. Watching the evolution of display advertising from early 2007 through late 2008 offers a unique perspective on the ebb and flow of the candidates as well as the issues that resonated with voters.

The presidential ad eruption began to bubble as early as January 2007. Democratic primary hopefuls including former North Carolina Senator John Edwards and popular early rivals Senators Hillary Clinton and Barack Obama placed ads on left-leaning political blogs such as MyDD. Clinton even ran ads promoting a live Webcast on conservative sites like Power Line.

Running ads on blogs was seen as an especially smart tactic for primary campaigns looking to score points with the parties' bases. Yet, McCain's online ad man, Eric Frenchman, cautioned that blogs were not enough. Around that time, on his Pardon My French blog, Frenchman suggested that Democratic candidates' "heavy reliance on social media and the lack of advertising via standard online advertising or even search marketing" restricted those campaigns to a small, perhaps narrowly focused audience. By "confining their online activities to heavy users of the blogosphere, they could be missing out on extending their message to folks that just aren't spending every minute toiling over blogs," he wrote.

In the meantime, Frenchman put the McCain money where his mouth was. The John McCain 2008 Exploratory Committee started out in January 2007 with video-enabled ads on AOL. The ads featured one of three 30-second videos presenting the candidate's points of view, and allowed people to submit e-mail addresses and other contact info within the ads themselves. It was an early effort intended to drive people to the official site to donate, but more important, to start building the campaign list.

"Be there from the start," said another ad seen on the conservative community and opinion site Townhall.com. The netroots building efforts were off and running.

"We've definitely seen more Republican activity, even for the [2006] state campaigns," said Rob Clark, PointRoll VP channel development. "It seems to be more a part of their DNA." PointRoll is the ad technology firm that enabled McCain's video ads.

Little did he and Frenchman know, but Obama for America eventually would become the most prolific online political advertiser in history, influencing campaigns for years to come.

The earliest display ads from presidential campaigns spotted last year by Nielsen Online were from three early frontrunners, Republicans McCain and Romney, and Democrat Clinton. McCain's early Web ad messaging had a decidedly different focus from that of its later days. In April 2007, around the time that McCain was stressing progress in Iraq and defending his "bomb-bomb-bomb-bomb-bomb-Iran" parody of the Beach Boys' classic "Barbara Ann," his campaign was running millions of Web ads declaring, "Surrender is not an option." Another often-seen ad referenced the candidate's experience and forthright reputation: "America Deserves Experience. America Deserves Straight Talk. McCain." The ads showed current images of McCain as well as photos from his days as a Navy pilot.

Yet, even in early 2007, the McCain Web team began experimenting with issue-based ads that featured cartoonish characters rather than sober shots of the war-hero candidate. "$74 million tax dollars for peanut storage costs? That's Nuts!" exclaimed an ad displaying silly images of peanuts with big pie-eyes. It went on: "$100 million tax dollars for citrus assistance? Orange You Outraged? $60.4 million tax dollars for salmon fisheries? Something smells fishy." The sole reference to McCain was the ad's "Paid for by John McCain 2008" disclaimer. Millions of McCain ads were seen on financial sites and conservative opinion and community site Townhall.com, among other sites.

Romney's camp recognized the importance of online advertising early on, too, running thousands of display ads featuring what became a mantra for the conservative's campaign: "Strong. New. Leadership." The ads asked voters to "Help Governor Romney Build a New American Dream," and were seen on National Review Online and FoxNews.com. The reference to Romney as "governor" indicated they may have been geographically targeted to Massachusetts residents, or residents of New England states who were more likely to know the Republican hopeful as a former governor, in an effort to build grassroots support in the early days of his primary campaign.

Clinton's campaign jumped in with ads on CNN.com that suggested voters "Join the Conversation." Other ads took an issue-oriented approach, inviting people to sign a petition to end President Bush's veto threat against Iraq War-related legislation.

Clinton's stance on the Iraq War funding legislation – which also set a deadline for withdrawal of U.S. combat troops in a year's time – put her in direct opposition to the president, as well as to McCain. White House spokeswoman Dana Perino called the legislation "defeatist." McCain was among a few senators who did not vote when the bill hit the floor.

The two GOP frontrunners – McCain and Romney – dominated the online political ad scene that spring. McCain carried on with his issue-oriented approach, with some ads focusing on pork-barrel government spending or the War in Iraq – both hot topics among the skirmishing army of Republican hopefuls.

Among the most frequently seen ads was one asking, "Sick of wasteful spending?" The ad told viewers to "Take our survey." Still, the McCain camp kept in line with his staunch war stance with a dominant "Surrender is not an option" ad message.

Traditional Republican issues were a focus for Romney, too. In expandable rich media ads, he featured issues such as taxes, supporting the military and wasteful government spending. Both campaigns reached out to the conservative base by placing their ads on right-leaning news and opinion sites like NewsMax, TownHall.com, and National Review Online – places they hoped would be ripe for the donation picking.

By June, immigration was front-and-center for Republicans. McCain was working with Democratic Sen. Edward Kennedy on an immigration reform bill. Not only were GOP hardliners annoyed by McCain's embrace of the liberal senator from the state they liked to call "Taxachusetts," they considered the legislation to be an amnesty for millions of immigrants living illegally in the U.S.

Tancredo dug right in with an aggressive immigration-related ad seen only on Drudge Report, widely considered to have a conservative leaning. The ad came just in time for a Senate vote on the divisive bill. Tancredo's ad demanded, "Defeat Amnesty Politicians." It linked to a petition declaring, "Here is my message for any politician who supports an amnesty bill: I will commit myself to working for your defeat!" It wasn't a stretch to consider the ad and the petition a direct attack on McCain.

Meanwhile, Romney ran millions of ads, some of which focused on "employment verification for immigrants," or used the slogan, "Strong Military. Strong Economy. Strong Families."

Democrat John Edwards peeked in with ads suggesting that Web users "Join the campaign to change America."

Around that time, the McCain campaign had been rattled by departures, staff switch-ups, and a lack of funding. Some online pundits speculated that the layoff of McCain's e-campaign manager Terry Nelson in July spelled doom for the campaign, despite the early stage of the primary season. Some also wondered whether a drop in his display ads was a direct reflection of those internal upsets.

Connell Donatelli's Frenchman said otherwise. "We're just reevaluating what we're doing," he said, noting the campaign had increased its search marketing effort because it found paid search to be effective and cost-efficient. "Summer is not exactly the best time to advertise," he added.

Much like many commercial advertisers, some of the presidential campaigns appeared to take a summertime siesta from Web advertising, although McCain did use Web ads to promote his tough-guy image as the summer pushed on. The straight-talk and pork-barrel spending messages were seen along with ads describing the candidate as "One Tough Guy, One Great Leader."

And, even though his Web campaign sometimes seemed disconnected from his offline messaging, McCain's "Surrender is not an option ads" were right in line with his "No Surrender" summertime tour theme.

The Romney camp also touted their candidate's strength and leadership qualities. Some ads expanded to show video and information about Romney's stances on conservative issues like taxes, the military, and wasteful spending. And some drew unwanted attention. Ads appeared on gay-oriented sites like Gay.com, PlanetOut and Advocate.com – not exactly where one would expect a conservative Republican to advertise.

A November 2007 New York Times story exposed the embarrassing episode, which the Romney campaign blamed on an ad network mix up. However, in explaining that some online political advertisers still didn't quite understand the nuances of online advertising, the article symbolized the political media's own common lack of understanding of online ad basics.

The article referred to ad networks as systems that "randomly" place ads across Web sites, or "randomly bombar[d] thousands of sites" with ads. The truth is ad networks are anything but random. Their key selling point is their ability to target specific audiences according to geographic, demographic, and other information. Political reporters glommed onto the campaigns' more accessible or easily hyped social networking tactics but rarely covered their online advertising efforts.

The Obama camp certainly understood ad targeting, though their ad messages were standardized, shunning issues and aiming to build grassroots support. Ads asked voters to "Sign Up for Invitations to Campaign Events" and prompted them to join other campaign supporters.

As the Iowa caucuses and early primaries closed in, Romney and McCain homed in on messages they hoped would resonate with the Republican base. McCain went from running ads with multiple messages to focusing mainly on his "No Surrender" slogan in September, hoping to exhibit the candidate's unwavering stance on the war in Iraq.

Romney aimed to rally supporters and establish a platform of popular conservative issues like curbing government spending and securing borders. Ads were strident: "Republicans Have to Get Our Own House in Order. Stop wasteful spending. Secure the borders. Insist on high ethical standards."

By October 2007, GOP candidates went on an online ad rampage, recognizing the Iowa caucuses and early primaries were creeping ever closer.

In ads seen on FoxNews.com, Republican hopeful Fred Thompson went after his GOP rivals Romney and Giuliani, using their own words to question their views on abortion – another important primary topic for the Republicans.

"I do not take the position of a pro-life candidate," read the ad, quoting an earlier pro-choice era Romney. Then came the Giuliani jab: "I'm pro-choice. I'm pro-gay rights." Finally, Thompson's stern visage appeared beside the phrase, "I was a proud conservative yesterday, I remain one today, and will be one tomorrow. Support the Real Conservative."

Thompson took the same tack in ads seen on right-wing blogs such as Power Line, Right Wing News, Right Thoughts, and Biblical

Womanhood. "This is not a time for philosophical flexibility, it is a time to stand up for what we believe in."

But Thompson's Web ad attacks and Tancredo's before them were nothing compared to what the McCain camp would have in store for the remainder of the election season. Before Obama emerged as the candidate to beat, McCain kept Clinton – the candidate conservatives loved to hate – in the crosshairs.

Clinton's own display ads were few and far between, but the McCain camp made sure she showed up in some anyway. A grinning, sunflower-adorned Hillary flashed the peace sign in one ad. "1 million for a Woodstock Museum? Not so groovy man," said the ad. It mirrored a McCain TV spot which alluded to Clinton's proposal to fund a museum in Woodstock, N.Y., commemorating the legendary drugged-out 1969 concert event. Other ads displayed the Vietnam veteran as a hard-as-nails foil to a hippie-fied Hillary.

That Hillary ad did pretty well, too. According to McCain ad man and prolific blogger Eric Frenchman, it was "one of the highest clicked ads for Senator McCain's campaign."

The ads were doing well enough for the McCain camp to keep using Clinton's name and face to their advantage. They recognized Clinton's ability to conjure conservative venom. "Is This The Future You Want?" asked an ad showing her face tottering to-and-fro inside a crystal ball. "Make Sure It Doesn't Happen!" Another ad displayed a giant newspaper headline that today can only remind political junkies of the Chicago Daily Tribune gaffe of 1948. This time, instead of "Dewey Defeats Truman" the ads declared, "McCain Beats Clinton, Read All About It!"

Yet another attack ad featured close-ups of Clinton and Obama. "Who do you trust to protect America?" they asked. Like many other McCain display ads, they made no reference to McCain aside from a tiny disclaimer.

The campaign also targeted GOP candidates Thompson, Romney,

and Giuliani, using their own words of praise for McCain against them. "If I wasn't running I'd probably be supporting him for president," went a Giuliani quote. "John McCain has shown the characteristics of leadership like no one else that I've ever seen," was a Thompson line from back in '99. A Romney quote called McCain "a great man." The ad quipped, "At least they agree on something. John McCain for President."

Meanwhile, Edwards and Obama were anything but confrontational. Obama ads encouraged voters to join his campaign and attend local appearances of the charismatic orator. Edwards ran a relatively small number of ads on MySpace, picturing the former 2004 Democratic vice presidential candidate in front of a gigantic American flag. "Join the campaign to change America," read the ads. Yep, it seemed like everybody was flying the change flag at that point in the election cycle.

Political ads aren't typically known for their impeccable design qualities or subtlety. Although many display ads created for the 2008 presidential campaigns raised the bar for political ads online, many weren't only stylistically challenged, but bordering on the bizarre.

Tancredo's "Defeat Amnesty Politicians" ad, screamed in red text on a white background, and looked somewhat cheap. Others such as Thompson's anti-Giuliani/Romney ads and some McCain ads were so loaded with quotes they seemed poorly planned from a design perspective. Some of McCain's ads, like the ones featuring googley-eyed fruit and Clinton in a goofy hippie getup, had an almost undignified quality that seemed antithetical to McCain's image.

But many of the ads grabbed attention. Take an especially eye-catching anti-war ad from Democratic hopeful Bill Richardson that were seen in December, just before the Iowa caucuses. "Continue war in Iraq until 2013? 2013! What the @$#!?" exclaimed the implicitly profane ad. "The cost of war is already too high," it concluded, prompting users to click through and visit www.2013istoolate.com. The ad included forecasts of the numbers of deaths, casualties and dollars to be spent on the war by 2013.

The weirdness continued for McCain toward the end of the year through an anti-earmark ad with a tongue-in-cheek message. A bear flapped his jaw open and closed, mouthing a one-liner McCain himself would repeat months later in a town hall-style debate with Obama. "Three million of your tax dollars to study the DNA of bears in Montana – I don't know if that's a paternity issue or a criminal issue," joked the ads, which were also seen throughout the general election season.

In stump speeches, and later on during the September 2008 presidential debate, audiences heard McCain goof on the bear DNA theme. "I don't know if that was a criminal issue or a paternal issue, but the fact is that it was $3 million of our taxpayers' money. And it has got to be brought under control," he quipped during the nationally televised debate.

Toward the end of 2007, the McCain campaign presented the candidate in a serious, heroic light in other ads that seemed like foils to the cartoonish bear ads. One that stood in stark contrast, for instance, was a video-enabled unit featuring a clip of the senator in his younger years as a prisoner of war in Vietnam. The "Courageous Service" video was one promoted by the campaign for months before.

Romney's campaign steered clear of silly ads, though there was something uncharacteristically fun about an ad effort launched in December. The Romney camp set a specific fundraising goal, calling it the Media Victory Fund. Display ads used pop-art style graphics and bold, bright colors, telling supporters to, "Tune in to Victory. Help Put Mitt Over the Top." The goal was to raise $1 million.

If any one word signified the 2008 presidential election, "change" was it. And, of course, Obama's campaign came to embody the term. But early on in display ad land, "change" didn't belong to just one candidate. In fact, Obama's ads didn't seem to embrace the "change" message until 2008.

In late 2007, Romney and Edwards both focused on "change" as an online ad theme. "Join the campaign to change America," said the Edwards ads. While Edwards played the change card from the left, Romney did it from the right. "Change Begins with us," was a tagline employed in a variety of ads from the outside-Washington candidate.

In December, Romney carried on with a new ad promoting his "clear vision of change for America." The ad told voters, "He did it in business, the Olympics, and in Massachusetts and He can do it in Washington." (Romney served as CEO of the Salt Lake City Olympic Games in 2002.)

By January, Obama's ads picked up the "change" torch and never looked back. Many ads that urged supporters to "Help Elect Barack Obama President of the United States" now were prefaced with the phrase, "Change we can believe in."

The majority of the ads placed by the Obama campaign at that stage of the cycle contained a simple message: "Meet Barack Obama. Sign Up for Invitations to Campaign Events," "Get to Know Barack Obama," "Attend Local Campaign Events." The ads didn't ask for donations, but the ultimate goal was to collect supporter e-mails for fundraising purposes.

The candidate's charisma and growing popularity enabled the campaign to rely on his image and a set of simple messages to inspire people to click through and visit his site to sign-up or donate.

Romney called it quits in early February, but before the end, his campaign ran ads with embedded video clips comparing his pro-life and pro-traditional marriage stances with those of Republican hopeful Mike Huckabee. It soon became clear that Huckabee's bid was, in effect, over as well.

As Obama focused on driving voters to the polls and collecting names via poll location finding forms, McCain continued taking aim at Clinton. The crystal ball appeared again in early '08, as did the "not so groovy" Woodstock ad. "McCain Beats Clinton" and "Who do you trust to protect America?" (also a poke at Obama) showed up, too.

Because McCain no longer had to battle Romney and Huckabee in state primaries, his campaign could go after the Republican base on conservative sites rather than buying ads on local sites as was done in more contentious months. Many of his ads were found on conservative sites like Washington Times, Newsmax, National Review, and Town Hall, as well as Web sites associated with conservative commentators like Lucianne Goldberg's Lucianne.com and David Horowitz's FrontPage Magazine.

It's no wonder many of those ads were focused less on McCain and more on Clinton, the nemesis of conservatives. McCain was struggling to win over conservatives who remained dissatisfied with his stances on issues such as immigration and campaign finance reform. When it came to drumming up donations and building his list, his campaign may have been better off getting their attention by threatening a Clinton dynasty.

McCain was out of the primary woods, but Obama had a series of important battles yet ahead. Texas and Ohio were right around the corner. The candidate began a display ad strategy he continued throughout the primaries and later before the general election. The week before the March 4 primaries in Texas and Ohio, Obama launched expandable video ads on the homepages of a variety of newspaper and TV station sites based in those states. Both Texas and Ohio allow voters to cast their ballots before primary day at locales like the county clerk's office; Obama wanted to take advantage of that.

Millions of standard display ads hit Texas and Ohio voters in February, too. In some ads, the Obama logo followed along as the user's cursor traveled over a cartoonish image of the Lone Star state. "Vote Now for Barack Obama. Find Your Early Vote Location," demanded the ads. Like the homepage video ads, they pushed users to a Web form to locate early voting places. Ads appeared on local sites like Austin's Statesman.com, Dayton Daily News, and ToledoBlade.com. Others were spotted on sites such as Politico and The Huffington Post.

The state-specific, "follow the bouncing Obama logo" ads were unique, but the newspaper homepage campaign was especially impressive. The ads looked good. Users were enticed to expand them to reveal a video message.

"Have you tried the convenience of early voting?" The ads prompted voters to "Find your early-vote location." Embedded video of TV spots mentioned issues like health care, the war in Iraq and middleclass tax cuts. Local media ad firm Centro placed the ads on behalf of the Obama campaign and designed the ad creative in-house.

The ads featured a variety of video spots. One centered on losing jobs overseas, the "misguided" Iraq war, and the chance for "a nation healed, an America that believes again." Another black-and-white video noted Obama's anti-war stance, his role in congressional ethics reform, and the potential to repair the country's poor perception internationally. Another ad featured a video about affordable health care, Iraq, cutting taxes for the middle class, and ending tax breaks for companies moving jobs overseas.

Users clicked through to landing pages featuring a close-up video message from Obama in which he asked people to enter their street address, city, ZIP code, and e-mail address to retrieve information about their closest early voting location. "I need you to do more than just vote," he told Texas voters, explaining their "Texas Two-step" caucus and primary voting process.

When the Clinton people caught a glimpse of the Obama ads, they were crushed. They recognized the amount of time and resources – and money – that goes into such a well-executed and innovative effort. The ads looked so cool, they wished they'd have pulled something off like that themselves (or had the buy-in from higher-ups to do something so stylish and obviously pricey). Picture a few Web staffers huddled around a computer with their jaws agape and you're probably close to capturing the actual scene.

Indeed, things weren't looking so hot for Hillary. Obama had won a string of 10 primaries and caucuses in a row between Utah on February 5 and Wisconsin on February 19.

"She's behind. Make no mistake. If she loses either Texas or Ohio, this thing is done," famed Democratic campaign strategist James Carville said in mid-February. Even Hillary's husband Bill, for whom Carville had helped win the presidency, told Lone Star state voters before their two-step primary and caucuses she'd be Texas (and Ohio) toast if she didn't win both states.

Despite a desperate need for Clinton to beat Obama in Texas and Ohio, her campaign ran no display ads. But, regardless of her ad scarcity and Obama's big Web ad push, Clinton beat Obama in both March 4 races. The Democratic race was thrown for a loop.

Though she squeaked past Obama in Texas, it was a total KO in Ohio, where she beat her opponent by over 10 points. The nomination was now too close to call. Democrats talked of a "Dream Ticket" pairing Clinton and Obama. The wins gave Clinton and her supporters a lifeline, but it had Democrats popping aspirins. They were supposed to know by now who their nominee would be!

After a big comeback (remember, that past summer the candidate had been practically left for dead), McCain was in a prime position to move ahead with his general election campaign. And his presumptive nomination meant the Democrats had to convince voters they could take him on in the general election, so they needed to focus on a McCain strong suit: national security and defense.

While Obama and Clinton squabbled over who'd be the toughest commander-in-chief, McCain had been pounding the idea that he would be the strongest leader into the heads of Americans for months.

"Who do you trust to protect America?" asked McCain display ads showing photos of the three candidates. While he hammered home on security in his display ads, the bulk of Obama's were still focused on getting people to visit his site and "Join Us," or on reminding people to vote in upcoming primaries.

The McCain Web team may have had some trouble integrating with the rest of the campaign, but in some ways their online ad messages were integrated, at least when it came to the issues. The McCain ad approach indicated a belief that Internet advertising could be used in conjunction with offline ads for persuasion, even if the main goal was fundraising. Obama's video-enabled ad splash in Texas and Ohio showed his camp also recognized the dual-use potential of Web ads; at least they were willing to experiment with the concept.

Around that time, Obama endorser MoveOn.org Political Action had introduced its "Obama in 30 Seconds" campaign. Just like they did in the previous presidential race, the left-wing group used the Web to solicit funds to buy television ads. In 2004, the goal was to promote the "Bush in 30 Seconds" TV ad contest, and this recent effort used much the same template: get people to vote online for television ad contest submissions.

The organization spent about $30,000 for video and display ads on YouTube and liberal blogs like Open Left, Crooks and Liars, and Talking Points Memo. "Decide which Obama ad we air on national TV? Yes. You Can," said the ads, parroting the familiar

Obama mantra.

If anything, the MoveOn campaign was yet another reminder that TV still rules in the minds of political advertisers, even for organizations that were born online. Web ads made sense as a promotional vehicle for MoveOn, considering that's where its potential supporters are. However, as MoveOn's head of research and development Daniel Mintz said, TV is still important. "Different media serve different purposes," he said, suggesting online advertising "may not always be the best use of resources."

The next big fight was for Pennsylvania. After months of neglecting online display advertising, Clinton came out swinging with a campaign aimed purely at fundraising in March. Ads urging viewers to make history by contributing to her campaign were seen on prominent news sites, including CNN, AOL News, Slate, and The New York Times.

The campaign used one basic message: "Help Make History. Support Hillary Clinton Today! Contribute $50 Now." The ad blitz coincided with e-mails signed by Bill Clinton: "Can you help put Hillary in the position to win Pennsylvania with your contribution today?"

Clinton asked for cash to pay for Web ads to target Pennsylvania voters. In April, a giant homepage image on her campaign site was dedicated to fundraising for specific types of ads, including radio spots, online ads, and even door hangers. "Help us recruit supporters and get out the vote in Pennsylvania with targeted online ads," read the plea. The goal was $2.5 million for TV and $100,000 for the Web.

The Web was clearly all about money for Clinton. But the Obama camp, yet again, was willing to try online display advertising to persuade voters. Targeting Keystone state residents, they launched issue-based ads portraying Obama as a leader on fuel efficiency. The ads appeared on Pennsylvania newspaper and TV sites such as PittsburghLive.com and Philly.com.

"Which presidential candidate refuses money from oil company PACs and their Washington lobbyists?" asked the ads. The campaign hoped to reach voters feeling the pinch of high gas prices, which dominated news headlines.

Clinton, McCain and Obama were pictured alongside a list of high gas station prices; a fuel pump whizzed across the ad, following the user's mouse. Scrolling over each candidate's image revealed a different message. Clinton and McCain were characterized as oil company donation recipients, while Obama came off as the clean candidate promoting clean energy.

The Obama energy ad told voters, "Hillary Clinton has taken more money from PACs and Washington lobbyists, including those for oil and gas, than anyone in the race. She voted for oil tax giveaways and against increasing alternative fuels." McCain was panned for accepting contributions from oil industry PACs and lobbyists.

Obama was the candidate who claimed to refuse money from big oil. The ad said "Senator Obama is a leader in fighting for higher fuel efficiency standards, alternative fuels, and for the repeal of tax breaks for oil companies." It linked to a page on Obama's site focused on energy and the environment. Along with videos on energy-related topics, information on his record, and goals for legislation on renewable fuel and higher gas-mileage standards, the page featured links to donate, sign up to volunteer, and visit the Pennsylvania for Obama page.

McCain's campaign soon would introduce the energy price issue into his own Web ads. But first they would run some of their quirkiest ads.

Harking back to another unexpected ad effort the previous March, the McCain camp ran ads promoting a college hoops contest. "Bracket Busted? Need a Second Chance? Create a New Bracket in the Second Chance Challenge," read the ads. Like the others centered on Clinton or pork-barrel spending, the ads barely mentioned the candidate. During the 2007 NCAA basketball playoffs, McCain's campaign site listed his bracket bets and urged supporters to register their team picks to win campaign gear.

Clinton won the Pennsylvania primary, but Obama's campaign continued its display ad barrage, and this time around lots of those ads were aimed directly at voters in the next battleground: North Carolina.

"One-Stop Early Voting April 17-May 3. Vote Now For Barack Obama," read millions of ads targeted to Tar Heel state residents. "You can register and vote at the same time, at a One-Stop Early Voting Location. NC.BarackObama.com. Find Your One-Stop Early Voting Location Now." North Carolina allows citizens to register and vote at the same time days ahead of election day. The North Carolina bombardment also continued into early May leading up to the state's primary.

While Obama virtually barnstormed North Carolinians, the Clinton camp carried on with pure fundraising, urging voters to contribute either $5 or $50 "Now."

In addition to Obama's hefty North Carolina ad push, the campaign targeted some ads to Indiana voters, though far fewer than were aimed at North Carolinians. "Indiana Early Voting is now open," the ads prodded. Obama won North Carolina by more than 10 points; Clinton won Indiana by a small margin.

McCain's ads didn't stray much from previous months, though there seemed to be a renewed focus on convincing people of his experience, leadership, and courage. "One man has the experience, One man has the courage, One man has our trust," read the most-seen ad. Another often-seen ad linked to McCain's "Courageous Service Video" of his heralded Vietnam War service.

By May 2008 the average price for a gallon of gas in the U.S. had skyrocketed to more than $3.70. Although many of the world's eyes were focused on the people of Myanmar after a devastating cyclone had washed away thousands early that month, Americans seemed more concerned with the price at the pump than anything else. McCain and Obama both attempted to use the domestic issue to their advantage.

The gas issue also helped them deflect attention from other topics such as Obama's former pastor, the Rev. Jeremiah Wright, whose fiery oratory and "God Damn America" sermon made national news. McCain had his own negative association to deal with. The left continued to paint him as a Bush doppelganger.

The high cost of getting around helped both steer voters away from those problematic issues. McCain went populist. He sought to appeal to everyday Americans in a series of messages focused on pocketbook issues. "Gas Prices Too High?" asked ads displaying metaphorical fuel prices on a gas station sign: "Arm. Leg. First Born." Like several of McCain's issue-related ads seen throughout the election season, they suggested users sign an online petition. In this case, the petition supported his gas tax moratorium proposal.

"You Need Help," stated another economic message ad from McCain, promoting "John McCain's Economic Plan, Immediate Help for American Families." The ads pictured a young couple seated at the kitchen table, poring over bills.

But McCain's campaign hadn't forgotten the need to attract conservatives. In addition to continuing long-running ads against pork-barrel spending, new ads touted the senator's support of "judges who will properly interpret the Constitution and not legislate social policy from the bench."

Like McCain, Obama's camp also ran ads about gas taxes but took the opposite side, and attacked Clinton for her support of a gas tax moratorium. "Beware of Hillary's Gas Tax Gimmick," cautioned some ads; others prompted users to view a video on "The Truth About Gas Prices."

Before ducking out of the race and endorsing Obama in June, Clinton continued asking supporters to "Help Make History" by giving either $5 or $50 donations.

In mid-summer, the National Organization for Women's PAC picked up Clinton's history-making mantle, suggesting that voters, "Change History." The ads were spotted on sites such as Home & Garden Television, SoapZone, Food Network, and Martha Stewart.

Iran was on the minds of many that spring, and the McCain camp saw an opportunity. Looking ahead to Iran nuclear talks and Obama's whistle-stop Mideast tour in June, McCain's campaign ran millions of Web ads featuring close-ups of Iranian President Mahmoud Ahmadinejad and Obama.

"Is It OK to Meet Unconditionally with Anti-American Foreign Leaders?" asked the ads. They alluded to Obama's 2007 statement that he would negotiate with Iran without conditions. Obama was also paired with Cuban leader Fidel Castro, a villain to many voters of Cuban decent in the swing state of Florida. "Barack Obama picks up another major endorsement," said ads showing a photo of Obama beside one of the aging leader. "Fidel Castro thinks he is 'the most advanced candidate.' "

McCain also stepped up messaging about the high cost of gasoline with new ads showing a thief dressed in a black mask and knit cap. "Are you being robbed at the pump?" asked the ads showing the crook clutching a gas pump. It prompted viewers to click and "Take the Survey."

Both camps targeted ads to voters in battleground states, including Pennsylvania, Florida, and Wisconsin. As McCain pushed new and well-worn issue-based ads and took swipes at his foe, Obama seemed to focus entirely on prompting supporters to join the campaign.

But Obama had backup.

Going negative wasn't Obama's style. So, while his campaign carried on its non-confrontational way, the Democratic National Committee and MoveOn poked at McCain's Achilles heel. Both groups aimed to equate President Bush with the Republican nominee. "Don't Give Bush a 3rd Term, Stop John McCain," declared DNC ads. The mission: donate $25 to pay for anti-McCain TV spots.

Meanwhile, MoveOn PAC took a slightly more tongue-in-cheek approach, implying how difficult it is to decipher Bush's words from McCain's. "While running for president, who called himself 'a different kind of Republican?' " asked ads prompting users to answer "Bush" or "McCain."

Summer 2008 brought with it an increasingly gloomy economic outlook, and McCain's ads affirmed his populist economic message, focusing mainly on exorbitant gas prices. "Have gas prices turned your vacation into a mirage?" inquired one ad. "Do gas prices have you stuck in park?" asked another. Most enticed people to sign an online petition.

Down ballot Republicans grabbed the gas message. Ads for Mitch McConnell, Republican senator from Kentucky, as well as for Pennsylvania Congressman Charlie Dent used gas prices to attract interested voters and donors. "Held at Gas Point?" asked Dent's ads. "Congressman Charlie Dent has a commonsense energy policy for America."

The DNC took the high-gas-prices road, too, with ads that told people not to get mad but "get registered."

Many of McCain's ads pounced on Obama and didn't show McCain at all. "It's great to have 300 advisors. But only one person can make the tough decision," noted one ad. Another displayed photos of Paris Hilton and Britney Spears, asking who the "Biggest Celebrity in the World" is. "The Answer May Surprise You," it said. The ad linked to content portraying Obama as a celebrity.

And yet again, the McCain ads represented a connection in some of his online and offline messaging. The "Obama as celeb" theme was rampant throughout McCain campaign rhetoric and television ads much to the chagrin of the Obama campaign.

"Only celebrities like Barack Obama go to the gym three times a day, demand MET-RX chocolate roasted-peanut protein bars and bottles of a hard-to-find organic brew—Black Forest Berry Honest Tea and worry about the price of arugula," declared McCain campaign manager Rick Davis in a July 30 e-mail to supporters.

Paris Hilton had the last laugh. In a popular Web video she implied she had better ideas on energy policy than Obama or McCain, and suggested – while lounging luxuriously in a skimpy bathing suit – maybe she'd make a viable candidate herself.

None of those newer attack ads made mention of McCain, besides in the fine print stating they were paid for by his campaign. The candidate's image, however, did appear in a large portion of ads that ran as the Republican Party looked ahead to its convention. Affirming a message that became a mantra of the September event, the ads pictured McCain, stars and stripes flowing in the background. "Country First Always," they proclaimed. "Donate Today."

The morning of the September 26 debate, McCain's Web ad team was caught with its tail between its legs. A display ad declaring McCain had won that evening's debate showed up on The Wall Street Journal site. The day before the Senator still hadn't agreed to participating in the debate. (He'd suggested the candidates hold off until Congress had passed its bank bailout bill).

The candidates duked it out till the very end online, with ads that went after specific audiences in important swing states. Sites across the Web were drowned in hundreds of millions of Obama's voter registration and state-targeted early voting ads in the final weeks.

Obama's campaign had shifted ad gears by September. The main focus was on getting people to register and vote early, and the ads reflected that. While most ads contained simple messages imploring folks to visit the VoteforChange site, some employed important issues like the economy and the War in Iraq to spark interest in registering and voting early.

"I'm voting because the economy stinks," said a young voter in a video-enabled ad. 'I'm voting to end the war," said another. "Whatever your reason, you don't need to wait till November to vote. Get everything that you need to vote early at VoteForChange. com," Obama said in the ad.

Obama's registration calls-to-action subsided as early voting ads gained strength in October. Florida residents were in the eye of that ad hurricane, which drenched them with hundreds of millions of early voting ads. "Florida Early Vote," and "Florida Vote by Mail," were among the ubiquitous messages. Voters in Ohio, Colorado, Iowa, Wisconsin, Indiana, North Carolina, and New Mexico were also hit. Many "vote early" ad elements moved or popped when scrolled over. Some used dynamic ad technology to display the current date.

The Obama campaign even targeted voters outside the U.S., telling them to "Vote from Abroad," in ads that sent them to Democrats Abroad, a Web site run by the Democratic Party. When early voting had ended, residents in Florida and other important states were told to "Find out where to vote. Get your polling place hours."

Meanwhile, McCain's display advertising had practically dried up as the election season came to a close. His Web team decided to throw its weight behind search advertising, which had been the most successful at driving signups and donations for McCain. But the display campaign did continue, focusing on issue-based messages for persuasion, and introducing what became strengths for the Republican ticket: Sarah Palin and Joe the Plumber.

Palin, the governor of Alaska, was a magnetic figure from the start when she hit the national stage at the end of August. After McCain named her as his Vice Presidential running mate, she'd managed in a matter of days to do what McCain struggled with for over a year: to solidify the Republican base. The self-proclaimed hockey mom and "commander-in-chief of the Alaska National Guard" struck a chord with small town and suburban voters, serving as a foil to the condescending caricature of Obama-as-celebrity.

Then there was Joe the Plumber. Himself a caricature almost from the moment McCain mentioned him during the last presidential debate, the Ohio plumbing contractor (real name Samuel J. Wurzelbacher) was used as a pawn by McCain and Obama as they battled on taxes. In the October debate, McCain had used him as a symbol of the entrepreneurial working man who could be negatively affected by Obama's tax plan if he decided to run his own business.

Joe the Plumber became synonymous with the tax issue, and was used more online in McCain and Obama search advertising than anything else. But his name appeared in some McCain display ads. "Are you 'Joe the Plumber'? Don't tax me for working hard," read one ad prompting people to "Learn More."

Throughout the election both camps targeted display ads to women. However neither ran ads with messages geared directly toward them until the final months, when both ran issue-based ads with themes important to women voters. The McCain camp had a leg up on the competition in that department with Palin. The campaign aimed to use her gender to their advantage in display ads that turned Palin into a brand representing female empowerment.

"They demanded change," read McCain/Palin ads displaying black-and-white images from the suffrage movement. Not only did they try to appeal to women's sense of history and franchise, they made Obama's "change" message their own – or tried to anyway.

One ad introduced in October featuring Palin showed a young girl in a field, her arms spread wide with optimism: "Inspiring a new generation of leaders," it said. Another praised Palin's debate performance, citing a quote from Wall Street Journal columnist Peggy Noonan: "She killed. It was her evening. She was the star."

Many of McCain's ads were spotted on women-centric sites such as iVillage and Better Homes & Gardens Online.

One of the things that drew McCain to Palin, or so we were told, was her reputation as a maverick. The hope was that Palin's no-frills, corruption-battling, outside-the-beltway reputation would reaffirm McCain's own persona as a maverick. Display ads showed Palin and McCain together, and deemed the candidates "The Original Mavericks."

After months of little to no attacks in their display ads, the Obama camp took a negative tone with their own women-aimed messaging. Abortion wasn't much of an issue during the election after the Republican primaries, and it wasn't much of one for McCain at all. In fact, the candidate – who believed exceptions for abortion should be made in the cases of rape, incest, or threats to a woman's health – didn't agree entirely with his party's platform, which called for a constitutional ban on abortions. So, when it came to wooing pro-choice women, the best the Obama camp could do was target the GOP platform, not the party's candidate.

"An alarming fact every woman should know. John McCain is running on a platform with a constitutional amendment to ban all abortions in America," declared one Obama ad. Another mimicked an Obama TV spot, implying McCain didn't support equal pay for women. "Women are paid 77 cents for every dollar a man makes. Only one candidate supports equal pay for equal work. Join Women for Obama."

The McCain campaign shot right back. "Obama talks big on Equal Pay for women. But the Women in His Senate Office Make $0.83 on the Dollar," said the counterattack, which called Obama "all talk."

Palin's image drove click-throughs for McCain/Palin fundraising ads asking donors to give $50 to the McCain Palin Compliance Fund. Similar ads placed online in earlier months asked for $25. The September fundraising mission was supported by Republican National Committee ads asking people to "Invest in Victory."

But by October, the McCain campaign was down to the wire, and its online ad team decided to throw almost all its weight behind search advertising. The few display ads it did run were focused on persuading voters that McCain was their man. New display ads with issue-based themes showed up, many prompting voters to "Learn More." An ad displaying images of wind turbines, solar panels and an off-shore drilling island read, "An all of the above energy solution."

Other economy-related ads pushed McCain's "Homeownership Resurgence Plan," and stated, "Your home is the foundation of your life."

Many McCain ads aimed to convince voters that Obama couldn't be trusted. "Obama says he didn't vote to increase taxes on people making $42,000 a year. But he did…Twice!" said one ad. Another tax-related ad noted, "Obama voted for higher taxes 94 times. Come On Senator, Tell the Truth." Those ads and others even used colors and other elements that had become synonymous with the consistent Obama ad style. Some McCain ads even featured the Obama logo.

The McCain team used Biden's words against him in ads that were most likely targeted to coal industry states such as Colorado, Indiana, Ohio, Pennsylvania, and Virginia. "No coal plants here in America. Build them over there [in China]," noted the ad, quoting a statement Biden made at a campaign stop in Ohio in late September. The ad decided the Obama-Biden ticket was "Wrong for America."

Both campaigns recognized Jews as an important voting bloc. For months the McCain camp ran millions of ads featuring Ahmadinejad's photo alongside Obama's, asking, "Is It OK to Meet Unconditionally with Anti-American Foreign Leaders?" Many of those ads were aimed at Jewish voters.

In the final months before the election, Obama's campaign hit back in the hopes of ensuring voters of Obama's dedication to defending the state of Israel. "As president, I will never compromise when it comes to Israel's security," stated ads that ran in The Jerusalem Post in September and October.

The Iraq War became a backburner issue toward the end of the election season, and the ads reflected that. However, MoveOn PAC kept the flame burning. "McCain to keep spending billions in Iraq while US economy tanks. Get the facts," said the ads. The liberal group also pushed for signups and donations through Obama sticker, button, and T-shirt giveaways promoted in display ads.

The "four more years' message, equating McCain with Bush, appeared in Obama ads, with support from Democratic National Committee ads linking to the DNC's JustMoreOfTheSame.com. "John McCain voted with George Bush 90% of the time. Learn More," read the ads.

Emily's List, an advocacy group that promotes Democratic women for office, also pushed for Obama along with two female candidates in his home state of Illinois. "High gas prices. Student loan debt. Health care costs. That's what I worry about. Barack Obama for Pres., Debbie Halvorson for House, Linda Holmes for IL Sen. They get my issues. They get my vote," said ads picturing a young woman.

Still, the thing on everybody's mind was the economy. The Dow was in the toilet. The NASDAQ had taken a nosedive. Layoffs were being announced left and right. The world's biggest banks were either collapsing or getting unprecedented federal assistance. People checked their 401K statements by squinting through their fingers.

Both candidates used the tax issue in display ads to promote their economic policies. "Let's be clear. Barack Obama will cut taxes for 95% of working families," read an Obama ad allowing people to enter their annual income to calculate their "Obama Tax Cut." They got their answer on a special tax calculator page on the Obama site.

The McCain camp referenced the Wall Street mess specifically. "Reduce Taxes & spending. Reform Wall Street. Restore prosperity," said the ads, demanding, "America Needs Economic Leadership."

On voting day as lines of voters curled around neighborhood schools and fire stations, both sides focused on getting as many supporters as possible to the polls. Prominent display ads on news sites in battleground states like Pennsylvania and Florida reminded voters to "Vote for Barack Obama." Although the RNC did some GOTV text messaging, there were no specific voting day display ads from the McCain camp.

**IRAK**

4,000 AMERICANOS MUERTOS

60,000 HERIDOS

**$600** MIL MILLONES GASTADOS

¿ESTAS REGISTRADO PARA VOTAR?

HAZ CLICK AQUÍ PARA VERIFICARIO

Is it OK to Unconditionally Meet With Anti-American Foreign Leaders?

YES    NO

PAID FOR BY JOHN MCCAIN 2008

Non-Expanded Ad

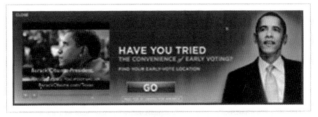

Expanded Ad

# GOOGLE WINS!

If you were to ask an online politico in 2004 what he thought of Kerry's or Bush's search ad strategy, you were more likely to get a blank stare than an opinion. They did next to nothing with search in the '04 presidential election cycle. It just wasn't part of the playbook.

How things have changed.

About 45 percent of Obama's online ad spending in the '08 race, around $7.5 million, went to Google. Even a bigger chunk of the McCain online ad budget probably ended up with Google. Practically every other political advertiser in '08 – from the primary candidates and national party committees to local sheriff campaigns – bought Google ads, too.

"I couldn't have done what I was doing without Google," an online ad strategist for one of the presidential campaigns said after the election.

The reasons for Google's appeal to political advertisers are no different from the reasons for its appeal to automakers, Web retailers, or mortgage lenders. The ad model represents what advertisers love about interactive advertising. The text-based search ads are simple to create. The ads are shown to people only when relevant. Advertisers can easily control and limit ad spending. And – perhaps most important for political advertisers

– they can readily tie ad expenditures to ad results. Just as the mortgage lender can determine the number of people who clicked a Google ad and filled out a loan form, the political campaign can track how many people clicked to sign a Web petition or donate, and determine how much each one of those sign-ups or donations cost.

McCain campaign search ad guru Eric Frenchman said he believed his own search ad efforts, as well as those of the Obama campaign, contributed to the candidates' primary wins by helping them build lists of potential donors. Commenting on his Pardon My French blog, Frenchman wrote, "We get $3 - $4 in donations for every $1 we spend online."

"Running ads on Google AdSense is a great way to stretch your ad dollars and offers demographic as well as content targeting that allows the small advertiser to act like a large advertiser," Frenchman wrote on his blog a week after the election in a post he called, "Confessions from a Google Ad Sense Junkie." He added, "because it can be credit card based and self-servicing, you can move the dollars around at lightning speed. Hence, the reason why political advertisers used it."

In addition to buying ads in Google's AdSense network and in Google search results, both camps bought search ads on Yahoo, MSN, and Ask.com.

McCain's campaign expenditure reports do not list individual media expenditures, so it is not possible to quantify his Google ad buys. But because Google garners the largest chunk of online search traffic, most of the political search dollars went there.

McCain and Obama also ran display ads through Google's AdSense network. They bought display ads directly from Web site publishers and through other ad networks, but a large amount of the millions of display ads seen across the Web were served through Google. The attraction for Obama, McCain, and other political advertisers is the same as with other advertisers. With Google, they pay only when a Web user clicks an ad, or takes an action such as donating or signing up for e-mail invites to speaking events.

"Obama as well as Romney ran a ton of money through AdSense," wrote Frenchman in his "Confessions" post. AdSense is Google's publisher network for text and display ads targeted to keywords in articles and other site content. "The McCain campaign... used it a lot, as did the RNC...but we focused more on search advertising."

Some of the Google and Yahoo ad spending had a trickle-down effect. Indeed, a portion of the money spent on their networks ended up in the hands of site publishers in those networks.

Google's head of political ad sales, Peter Greenberger, affirmed in mid-2008 that all of the presidential campaigns had or were running Google AdWords at the time. "[A]ll of them, too, have shown ads on our partner network [a.k.a. AdSense], and the investment is split between the two," he said in June 2008.

Greenberger lamented the Clinton campaign's comparatively limited use of search advertising. Her campaign spent about $292,000 on Google between March 2007 and April 2008 (before dropping out of the race in early June). A source familiar with the campaign's online ad strategy says most of her Web ad money went to search, not display.

"We tried everything," said Greenberger, "but basically as with any campaign with a finite amount of resources, there were internal discussions about the best use of those resources... I believe it was to their detriment, and I think that their money would have been better spent on media that had a direct return [as opposed to TV buys]."

The big role Google advertising played in Obama's digital marketing strategy couldn't have gone unnoticed by Google CEO Eric Schmidt, who – on a personal basis – was a vocal Obama supporter during election season.

# THE EMERGENCE OF SEARCH

Google scored big during the '08 elections, and it's a logical guess that a significant portion of the millions the search behemoth brought in went toward paid search ads on its own Web site. Yahoo, MSN, and Ask.com also received political ad dollars. While search advertising was barely on the radar for political campaigns just four years ago, most political or advocacy campaigns with any tech savvy ran paid search ads during the 2008 election season.

Search matters to political advertisers. It's relatively inexpensive. Like other performance-based ad buys, they can easily limit ad spending. Plus, they need only pay when someone clicks on an ad or performs an action such as providing an e-mail address or donating.

In addition, the targeting is unlike that of any other form of advertising. Because the ads show up only when relevant to a person's search, a campaign can be there when a potential supporter is looking for information on the candidate or issues such as off-coast drilling or Iraq. The ads can also be used to refute negative attacks from opponents.

The Obama team almost always used search in conjunction with its display ad campaigns. Search ads targeted nationally were used as a cost-effective means of fundraising, garnering signups, and counteracting negatives. In battleground states, search ads were a way to assist in field organizing efforts by attracting volunteers. Search ads for voter registration and early voting ads were targeted down to the voting precinct level in some cases.

People are increasing their use of search engines in general. The Pew Internet and American Life Project reported in August 2008 about the rise in search engine usage since 2002. Almost half of all Web users use search engines on a typical day; that's up from about a third of users in 2002.

Underscoring that increase, the percentage of Web users who search on a typical day grew 69 percent between January 2002, when Pew first tracked search activity, and May 2008.

A significant amount of Obama online advertising dough went to Google, but a lot of that money was spent on display ads placed through the firm's AdSense network. The McCain campaign did AdSense, too, but favored paid search. Not only were McCain's Web people big believers in search, there were even more practical reasons for their focus on search over display advertising.

The campaign drew money from three pots: McCain Palin 2008, the McCain Palin Compliance Fund, and McCain-Palin Victory 2008 (a joint fundraising committee formed by the Republican National Committee and the McCain-Palin Compliance Fund, and other Republican Party organizations).

The Compliance and Victory funds were set up to help the campaign cope with public financing regulations. The campaign's legal team put restrictions on how some of the funds could be used when it came to paying for display advertising, but all three of those funds could be and were used toward search ads.

It's no wonder Frenchman tooted his own search horn the day before the general election, calling the McCain search campaign "the greatest and most thorough search marketing campaign in the history of politics." On his blog he wrote, "When the undecided people turn to the internet to research their vote…. Our search efforts for Senator McCain will be there to direct them to the right information they are looking for to make the decision to vote for Senator McCain."

While search ads were used throughout the election season to steer voters toward educational information about the candidates, to help them find nearby polling places, to promote local events, or to counteract smears, the main reason for using search was – you guessed it – list building to facilitate fundraising.

Most candidates "are still really focusing on using search to solicit e-mail addresses and contributions," affirmed Bassik in July 2007. Many focused on targeting ads to keywords associated with the issues that generated the most action for the least amount of money.

"Hopefully, candidates will realize how valuable search marketing can be," said Bassik, a longtime evangelist promoting the use of digital media by political campaigns. "It delivers information directly to a motivated voter actively searching for information on a candidate."

In a July 2007 report from search engine marketing firm iCrossing aimed to assess the search ad prowess of the primary candidate campaigns. The company estimated the amount of money spent by the campaigns on search, and concluded that the McCain camp was using its search ad dollars most efficiently.

While such reports offer only a snapshot of the overall election season search landscape, they're worth considering. For instance, the iCrossing report from Spring 2007 provides an indication of how advanced the McCain camp's search advertising efforts were. Despite accounting for an estimated 29 percent of issue-based paid search ad spending in May compared to Edwards' 64 percent, McCain came out way ahead. In terms of visibility, McCain's paid search ads appeared more prominently than others in search results for a variety of issue-based terms: "stem cell research," "pro-life," "campaign finance," "electoral reform," "ethics reform," "government accountability," "government reform," "lobbyist," "special interests," "tort reform," "DNC," and "RNC."

In comparison, Edwards' ads were highly visible only in results for searches on "Iraq" and "war in Iraq." If his campaign did, indeed, spend twice as much as McCain's, they got far less bang for their buck.

iCrossing analyzed over 100 election-related issue keywords to determine which official campaign Web sites had a search presence.

Search ad spending by Romney comprised 3 percent among the candidates. Still, his ads were relatively prominent in results for "ethics," "family values," "war in Iraq," and "social conservative." Obama's campaign accounted for 4 percent of spending, and his ads were spotted in searches for "Iraq" and "war in Iraq."

About a year later, iCrossing reported that the McCain camp was the clear frontrunner in paid search, accounting for an estimated 60 percent of the total spent by the Obama, Clinton and McCain campaigns combined. Obama came in with 25 percent, while Clinton paid search represented 15 percent. Just how much that translated to in actual dollars was unclear, though.

The McCain camp also did the bulk of issue-based search ad spending among the three hopefuls, buying keywords like "abortion," "border security," "campaign spending," "Republican nomination," and "universal health care."

"I thought the McCain campaign actually did a better job of issues targeting using search," said Campaign Grid CEO Jeff Dittus after the election.

In January 2008, before the primary battles in Michigan, Nevada, South Carolina, and Florida, McCain's ads were dominant in searches related to state-specific keywords. His ads showed up in search results for "Michigan primary," "2008 primary Michigan," and "Republican primary Michigan." They touted his 2000 Michigan Republican primary win, along with an endorsement by The Detroit News."McCain Won Michigan in 2000, with Your Help, He Can Again."

McCain ads were spotted in South Carolina-related searches, too. Ads led users to a page featuring a video ad, and links to information on locating primary polling places and how to vote absentee. Half of the e-mail signups the McCain camp collected organically (as opposed to through buying lists) came through search efforts, according to a campaign insider.

Unlike McCain's ads, Romney's Michigan-related search ads were more generalized, mirroring messaging seen in his display advertising. Ads told supporters to "Sign Up and Join Team Mitt. Strong. New. Leadership."

Giuliani ads appeared in results for Florida-related searches. (Political junkies will recall the ex-New York City mayor's campaign put most of its eggs in the Florida primary basket.) Rudy for President ads declared "Strong Leadership. Proven Results" and led users to a donation page.

Obama also ran Florida search ads, despite a pledge not to campaign there because the state broke the Democratic Party's rules on holding early primaries. Ads in search engine results for "Florida Democrat primary" contained standard campaign messaging aimed at list-building: "Sign-up now for opportunities to volunteer and attend campaign events."

Republicans seemed to neglect Nevada's caucuses, which were expected to make a difference for Democrats. After scoring an endorsement by the casino state's large Culinary Workers Union, the Obama camp used search ads to help potential voters get to the polls. Just like the display ads reminding Nevada voters "to caucus for Barack Obama on Saturday at 11:00 a.m.," the search ad message was localized. "Find out where to caucus for Barack

Obama on Saturday, Jan. 19," read one ad linking to a form on Obama's "Nevada Headquarters" site.

Although they provide a glimpse into what voters might have seen when they searched for information on health care, the Iraq War, or a candidate, such reports are not a precise representation of how the campaigns used search advertising. There is little comprehensive data available to offer a reliable view of how or where the campaigns used search ads.

For instance, it was clear that many presidential search ads were targeted to specific states or ZIP codes during the primaries and the general election season. The best observers could do was rely on sporadic reports or conduct their own searches, which provided an obscured view because campaigns often targeted certain ads only to certain states. Also, sometimes an ad effort (search or display) appears for just a few days and then disappears before human or machine monitors can note it.

One thing we can be almost certain of is that the campaigns were buying their own candidate's names. Even when an official campaign site is well optimized and appears near or at the top of search results, "there's a certain degree of comfort people have clicking on the sponsored link," suggested Mike Turk, a tech consultant for Republicans.

It's also clear that the McCain campaign was dedicated to search. In June 2008, Google political ad man Peter Greenberger referred to McCain's mid-2007 malaise following a series of campaign staff departures and changes: "Even in the darkest days of the [McCain] campaign... they never stopped spending on Google AdWords. There were times, corresponding to the political polls, when maybe interest waned in his campaign, but he was ready to capture interest."

In late summer 2008, the McCain campaign was garnering lots of online donations through paid search efforts. According to Frenchman, August was the campaign's most successful month when it came to fundraising using search ads. "In the three days including [Sarah Palin's August 29 nomination day] we generated 220% more donations than the 28 days prior and… August was already our best month," he told his blog readers after the election.

The surge of interest Palin generated for the campaign – from fans and detractors alike – made for high search volume. "She was extremely popular in search activity and remained so until the very end," wrote Frenchman. "Prior to Gov. Palin, we used to run search advertising campaigns to drive people to come to events. That was only done once after her selection to be McCain's running mate."

McCain and Obama (along with the DNC) had been running Web ads with economic messages, many hinging on the high price of gasoline, for quite some time. As election day neared, it was clear the most important issue for voters was the economy.

Frenchman had decided to shift most of the display ad money into search. Then, a day or two after the October 15 presidential debate, he recognized a big opportunity to deploy that money. Using his experience running search for financial services firm HarrisDirect as his guide, Frenchman began buying thousands of brokerage- and investment-related keyword search terms.

"We were the first ones to jump on the Joe The Plumber issue online and, based on my past brokerage experience with HarrisDirect, I created a mini-online brokerage search campaign. I saw quite a number of blog posts from people commenting on our ads on stock tickers and other brokerage terms," he noted in a post-election blog entry.

"Barack Obama's Record. See the truth on how Obama's record compares with Obama's rhetoric," said the ads. Frenchman, who was also in charge of the national Republican Party's search advertising through his work with Connell Donatelli, also ran search ads linking to the GOP site. "Visit the GOP's post debate poll to vote John McCain winner of the debate!"

Frenchman offered some insight into his strategy before the

election on his blog: "Within minutes after becoming a debate topic, we put it into the search campaign sending it into our Rhetoric versus Record landing pages....The advertising competition around Joe the Plumber keywords is now very very fierce but I wonder if some of these advertisers have [the] budget to hang in there," he added, noting a variety of commercial advertisers had also jumped on the Joe the Plumber bidding bandwagon (many were actual plumbing contractors).

After the election, he acknowledged another obstacle to Joe the Plumber keyword ownership: "We ran up against Obama's tax calculator." The day before the debate, Obama's Web team launched an online form allowing people to submit income and tax filing status to determine how much money the campaign's proposed tax plan might save them. After the debate, Obama's search ads hitched a ride on the Joe wagon, renaming the tool, "Joe the Plumber's Tax Cut Calculator."

One Obama camp insider said the tax calculator ads probably helped to blunt the McCain campaign's Joe the Plumber tactics. However, according to the insider, although the tax calculator – which was also promoted through television ads – may have helped the Obama narrative regarding the economy, the ads may not have had much impact.

The McCain team had an online ad veteran with solid commercial ad experience in Frenchman. But the Obama camp had multiple people working on search keyword strategy. Some observers wonder whether a lack of integration hindered McCain's online campaign, including the paid search efforts.

Obama's digital staff, it seems, liberally shared information with their fellow teammates. For instance, a consultant handling search ad efforts associated with the Democrats' nominating convention was handed a detailed spreadsheet from the Obama campaign beforehand. There were lists of terms not to bid on and lists of search terms that should be bought. The concept was simple: Let's not compete for search keywords, which will only result in bidding up the cost of those keywords. Let's coordinate.

(Search advertising is sold through an auction-based system; the higher the bid, the more likely an ad will get prominent placement alongside relevant search results or article content.)

"We wouldn't want the campaign to buy the keyword 'Barack Obama' and have the convention buy it too," explained the consultant. "The spreadsheet was very instructive."

The McCain campaign didn't provide much direction to its Web team on keyword strategy, or which search and display ads should run or be pulled.

Not only do some suggest McCain's Web people were cut off from the rest of the campaign team, other Republican Web campaigns may have suffered for lack of communication with McCain's Web people.

"We competed against the McCain campaign for the [search keywords] in the congressional races, and that to me was a joke," said Campaign Grid's Jeff Dittus, who ran online ads for several 2008 Republican Senate and House campaigns. He had no luck when contacting local party leaders, asking if they could work together by sharing ad landing or destination pages or coordinating regarding keyword plans. "All we were doing was bidding up the words for lower taxes," he said after the election.

To be sure, such anecdotal examples don't necessarily mean the McCain campaign's Web team never communicated with the rest of the campaign, nor do they necessitate Obama's campaign was always a beacon of Borg-like interconnected bliss.

The Obama search team had its own keyword bidding battles. Especially when targeting ads to battleground states, they were up against corporate marketers, the Republican Party, the McCain campaign, T-shirt and sticker retailers, and even a big Obama endorser MoveOn. As the election drew near, it cost the campaign more and more to stay ahead as advertisers bid-up popular keyword prices.

In March 2008 search marketing consultants speaking at the Politics Online Conference, an annual must-attend event for Web politicos held by George Washington University's Institute for Politics, Democracy & the Internet, analyzed the Obama camp's approach to search. They'd noticed a lot of people had been Googling (or Yahoo-ing) things like "Is Barack Obama a Muslim?" The false Muslim association wasn't the first untruth the Obama campaign would have to contend with, nor would it be the last.

The consultants suggested the campaign could improve search engine optimization to ensure better rankings on results pages, by doing things like creating more specific titles for ad landing pages. But they did think the Obama team scored points for linking to a relevant page when people searched on terms related to the Obama/Muslim rumor. The page that popped up in results at the time called him a "committed Christian," and included video and text supporting that.

Optimizing Web site pages to appear high up in search engine results, however, takes time and effort – and sometimes a strong dose of sheer luck. Another way to do it more readily is by paying to make sure relevant links get special treatment. To refute negative attacks from opponents or spread by viral e-mails, the Obama campaign did just that.

About a month before the general election, a search on "Obama Muslim" turned up a sponsored link stating, "Barack Obama is a Christian. Get the facts at his official site."

At the same time, the Republicans were criticizing Obama for his connection to Weather Underground co-founder William Ayers. The Obama camp aimed to counteract those attacks through paid search, too. Results for searches like "Obama domestic terrorist" or "Obama Ayers" turned up ads for a campaign site dedicated to battling attacks or untruths. A sponsored result linking to Obama's FightTheSmears.com declared, "Obama Ayers Connection? …Don't Believe the Lies. Get Facts About Anti-

Obama Swift Boating."

Ayers-related searches also resulted in ads that seemed even more adamant: "Obama is not friends with William Ayers. Learn the truth & fight back." Those weren't from Obama's campaign, though. They came from the original target of "swift boating," 2004 Democratic presidential candidate John Kerry.

In October, rather than beg for online donations to buy TV ads – the standard tactic of most political campaigns – Kerry's leadership PAC had asked supporters outright to donate money to pay for Google ads. The goal was to reach undecided voters curious about Obama's alleged attachment to Ayers, domestic terrorism, or socialist thought.

"Right now, so many people are looking for the truth about the McCain smears that our ads are only reaching less than half of them," lamented an e-mail from Kerry's Campaign for Our Country PAC. "We need to put more resources behind the truth so every single person looking for answers sees our link to the real story about Barack Obama, and clicks on that instead of a link to a smear from a rightwing site."

The e-mails were sent to people who had signed up to receive messages from the PAC and his '08 Senate campaign. Some who had registered with his '04 presidential campaign also got the e-mail plea.

"Your donation by itself can make the difference in a close state like North Carolina, or Indiana, making sure some critical voters see the truth," noted the fundraising e-mail. "If you give just $50, that will pay for 140 people who click through to our pages and see the truth."

The Kerry search ads linked to TruthFightsBack.com, a site that "tracks, debunks, and counters the smears against Democrats." The site featured forms for submitting e-mail addresses and reporting smears. But its primary goal at the time wasn't to build a contact list; rather, it was squarely aimed at informing undecided voters about the Democrats' side of the story in the final days before election day.

"In this final stretch, it's particularly important that political advertisers are online to set the record straight about their candidate and perhaps persuade remaining undecided voters," Google's head of political ad sales Peter Greenberger said.

Yet, even the search ad-loving McCain campaign chose not to use paid search to combat attacks.

While Obama was fighting the Ayers left-hooks, his campaign was jabbing back. It was the perfect time to bring up McCain's connection to Charles Keating and the Savings and Loan scandal of the late 1980s – just as bank bailouts and failures were dominating the news headlines. People searching for Keating-related information were served sponsored links to McCain. KeatingEconomics.com. The site aimed to link McCain to financial crisis, and featured a video and other information connecting him to the former chairman of the Lincoln Savings and Loan Association, who was indicted on criminal fraud charges in 1990.

While the Obama camp probably would have used search to deflect the negative association, the McCain camp thought a Keating search effort would be counterproductive. They knew people were searching to learn more about the McCain/Keating connection. But instead of giving news media and bloggers another reason to write about it, they chose to remain silent when it came to paid search or defensive Web sites.

In mid-October, one of a series of reports on election-related search strategies from search engine marketing firm SendTec accused the McCain campaign of missing the opportunity to push the Ayers issue using search. It noted, "The McCain campaign is not bidding on any terms relating to [William] Ayers."

Maybe they weren't. But the Republican National Committee was. Ayers-related searches turned up paid links to the RNC's

BarackBook.com, a Facebook spoof naming Ayers as a member of Obama's "Friend Feed." The McCain campaign and the RNC used the same firm – Connell Donatelli – to handle its online ads.

# TARGETING LOCAL AND NICHE AUDIENCES

"It was clear immediately that Obama had not only a national fundraising strategy, but also had a targeted primary strategy to get-out-the-vote, target e-mail, and recruit volunteers," said a political consultant observing the presidential campaigns online.

National ad buys on Google and elsewhere fueled volunteer signups and donations, while ads placed on local sites or targeted geographically before the primaries and November election were used to push voter registrations and turn out the vote.

In the 2008 primaries, presidential campaigns experimented with local targeting like never before. They continued to buy ads on newspaper and television Web sites. But many of their local ad dollars went toward targeting Web users in key states and regions through ad networks like Google, AOL's Advertising.com, and on large portals such as Yahoo.

Targeting locally via ad networks was especially important to Republican Mitt Romney's campaign in the primary season. "We're primarily very focused on geo-targeting," Romney campaign e-strategy director Mindy Finn said in January 2008. "We want to own, so to speak, the inventory for a certain state."

As early as August 2007, months before the first big showdown in Iowa, McCain's and Romney's campaigns both ran display ads on local content sites. Romney ads were spotted on ClickOnDetroit.com and MySanAntonio.com, as well as sites based in Des Moines, Raleigh Durham, Phoenix, and New Orleans. McCain ads were aimed at early caucus and primary voters on DesMoinesRegister.com and South Carolina's TheState.com.

In December, when the Democratic primary field was still crowded with contenders, Bill Richardson's campaign customized ad creative for Iowa Caucus goers. "The war in Iraq has cost Iowans $3.5 billion," read one Richardson ad, linking to TheDifferenceOnIraq.com. The campaign even pushed a specific event in Des Moines in ads suggesting that voters "Join former U.N. Ambassador and Nobel Peace Prize nominee Governor Bill Richardson for a speech on the crisis in Pakistan." (Former Pakistan Prime Minister Benazir Bhutto had recently been assassinated.)

Obama won the test in the first of the long season's battles and used targeted online ads with Iowa caucus-related messages as part of the strategy. One promoted a precinct finder, caucus FAQ, student center and local Obama events.

By the time the primaries were really heating up on the Democratic side, McCain had pretty much sealed the deal on the Republican nomination. His almost guaranteed nominee status meant his campaign didn't need to focus too much on targeting voters in primary states.

Clinton did need to reach primary state voters. But her campaign didn't do much online advertising targeting them. In fact, the display advertising that appeared from time to time – besides being entirely fundraising oriented – was purely national in scope.

Some search efforts were targeted locally, though. The Clinton camp aimed search ads at voters in primary states like Pennsylvania and made sure residents of certain states clicked-through to state-specific pages on the campaign site.

Still, the mission was to exploit the Web through those ads as well as e-mails in order to raise funds for local TV spots and GOTV efforts.

Obama took a different approach to local during the primaries and beyond. While the others merely asked for signups and cash, Obama wanted votes, and he wanted them early. The video ads that showed up on Texas and Ohio news site homepages were among the more innovative – and pricey – of his local get out the vote efforts.

For about a week before the contentious March 4 Texas and Ohio Democratic primaries expandable video ads were placed on 22 newspaper and TV station site homepages, including on DallasNews.com, The Waco Tribune-Herald's WacoTrib.com, and The Akron Beacon Journal's Ohio.com.

In March 2007, WorldNow chief revenue officer Adam Gordon stressed the significance of the network effect in facilitating the campaign's broad regional media buy. "It speaks to the need for aggregation," he said. "That's why you see a big trend in the industry moving towards partnerships to scale.... Aggregation empowers advertisers to work with local stations the same way they partner with a national URL site." Many of the ads ran in WorldNow's network of local sites.

The ads took a localized approach to what the Obama camp had done throughout the lengthy primary season. All along, the grassroots-driven campaign ran Web ads aimed at collecting supporters' contact info and cash. In this case, because Ohio and Texas both supported early primary voting, the ads urged people to vote before primary day and find their closest early voting locations. "Have you tried the convenience of early voting? Find your early-vote location," the ads said.

And, since early voting in the Lone Star and Buckeye states ended before the ad effort did, the ads were altered to reflect the close of early voting, enticing voters to find their local polling place. Additional standard display ads promoting early voting were targeted to Texas and Ohio voters through online ad networks and showed up on sites like Austin's Statesman.com, Dayton Daily News, and ToledoBlade.com.

If that big push to convince Ohioans and Texans of "the ease and convenience of early voting" worked, it didn't get out enough of the vote for the candidate who paid for it. Clinton won both primaries.

The Obama camp carried on with its state-targeted GOTV efforts. "To vote for Barack Obama in the Indiana primary you must be registered to vote by April 7," stated an ad spotted on IndyStar. com and FortWayne.com in April. A similar ad aimed at South Dakotans in June reminded them that "Polls Are Open On Tuesday 7AM-7PM." Those were seen on sites like AberdeenNews.com, ArgusLeader.com, and ABC's Sioux Falls station site.

Clinton won in both states, but by the time the South Dakota primary rolled around, Obama had all but clinched the nomination. Even so, his campaign kept up the GOTV ad onslaught. "Remember to caucus for Barack Obama on Saturday at 11:00 a.m.," said ads aimed at Nevada voters.

The ads weren't successful in driving enough Obama voters to the polls; Clinton won Nevada, too. But maybe that wasn't the point. Had the Obama Web team only used primary outcomes to gauge the success of those localized ad efforts, they may have deemed them ineffective. After all, that video ad buy in Texas and Ohio was a pricey one. Their candidate didn't win, but the campaign continued to target ads to voters in other primary states months afterward, using customized get-out-the-vote messaging.

Just when it seemed to one media executive assisting in the local ad buys that the campaign had satisfied their primary state targeting needs, a cryptic e-mail subject line appeared in his inbox:

"Guam?"

His next task would be to help the Obama camp reach voters

in the typically neglected U.S. territory's primary, held in early May. Puerto Rico voters would also see GOTV ads before their primary in June. Obama won by a hair in Guam, but Clinton steamrollered past him in Puerto Rico, grabbing over 65 percent of the vote.

So, why bother running the ads if they didn't always help the campaign score a primary win? Because, when people clicked-through, they filled out a form to determine their nearby voting location, or signed up to receive e-mail or mobile alerts, or donated. The GOTV message was secondary, or at least complementary, to the ultimate goal of scoring contact information and cash, both essential for a post-primary push.

As the general election neared, battleground states were the next ad stomping grounds for the McCain and Obama campaigns. Even early on, the campaigns targeted ads to voters in closely watched swing states including Pennsylvania, Florida, and Wisconsin. Obama ads appeared on sites like Philly.com, Cincinnati.com, St. Petersburg Times-affiliated TampaBay.com, Pittsburgh's Post-Gazette.com and Madison's Channel3000. McCain ads were seen on Florida, Wisconsin, and Pennsylvania sites.

The McCain campaign flipped back and forth among states, counties, cities, congressional districts and ZIP codes, switching search and display ad targets based on polling or other campaign needs. Search ads were aimed at supporters in surrounding areas when the McCain caravan rolled into town for a rally or speaking engagement in the hopes of luring them to events.

By August 2008 the DNC and Obama campaign were working together online, sending out ads to voters in several swing states. They began using joint funds to run the ads, with an eye towards spurring voter registrations. "Register To Vote For Barack Obama And Other Candidates For Change," was the mantra in ads "Paid for by the Democratic National Committee and Obama for America and Authorized by Obama for America."

The ads went out to voters in swing states, including Florida, Georgia, Illinois, Michigan, Missouri, New Mexico, Nevada, North Carolina, Ohio, South Carolina, and Virginia, and many appeared on local radio station sites.

But the ad buy had unintended consequences: Ads showed up on raunchy Clear Channel rock radio station sites. Macon, Ga.'s Q106.FM and Harrisonburg, Va.'s 98rockme.com were among several Clear Channel sites that ran the voter registration ads alongside promos for "Celebrity Tramp Stamps" and links to content with lascivious labels like, "Red Light Girls," "Chicks on Toilets," and "Thong of the Day." Probably not the best place for a smiling Obama to reside.

At least a portion of the ads were placed by local media firm Centro, which was paid over $1 million by the Obama campaign in 2008. The Chicago firm places local online advertising for national advertisers. The ads came down from the offending sites soon after the company learned of the placements.

Ad placement mishaps aside, the voter registration ads were novel in that they marked the first instance of a disclosure naming both a party and a presidential candidate campaign in a Web ad during the 2008 election season. That may have been the only unique component of the ads, though. In keeping with his consistent message, they looked like most other Obama ads, featuring a bright blue background, prominent image of the smiling candidate, and the Obama logo.

The Obama camp, along with the DNC, kicked up their voter registration ad targeting to the next level. Just like the state-specific primary ads reminding voters when polls were open in their state, a series of slick Flash-based ads hit residents in Colorado, North Carolina, Pennsylvania, Missouri, Florida, Michigan, and other battle grounds after Obama's nomination. They were aimed at people who were not registered to vote in November. Some were created through dynamic ad systems that assemble customized components of ads according to the geographic location of the Web user about to see them.

However, many were pre-built and targeted to voters in specific states via ad networks. For instance, some September and October battleground-state ads geared toward voter registration, early voting, and  fundraising were targeted through networks according to demographics and designated market area filters.

On election day, Philly.com visitors and MiamiHerald.com readers saw last-minute expandable Obama ads on the homepages of those sites. They looked a lot like the earlier Texas and Ohio primary video ads. This time around, though, the election swung in Obama's favor.

Ad targeting, especially in today's data-centric world of political campaigning, goes way beyond location. It's about getting in front of groups and sub-groups of voters who are either likely supporters or are possible undecideds.

Early in 2007, behavioral targeting technology firm Tacoda began reporting data on visitors to presidential campaign sites, the idea being to find places on the Web to reach likely supporters – places that were less obvious spots for political ads. The company found, for instance, that Clinton supporters dug horror flicks and were in the market for full-size vans. Obama site visitors were indie film fans with Blackberry addictions and penchants for luxury cars.

Clinton's site visitors were over 30 times more likely to look at news content dealing with legal topics than all Web users. Obama's site visitors were only about nine times as likely to do so.

The main reason the data was presented was to show the presidential campaigns that there's more to online political advertising than running banners on news sites.

McCain and Obama were all over the news sites. Obama bought on Politico and The Huffington Post. McCain was on right-leaning news sites like Newsmax. Both were on scores of newspaper and television station sites through ad networks and local media buys.

But their ads showed up in some unlikely spots throughout the election. Take the recipe sites. Yes – the recipe sites. Obama ads appeared month after month on the decidedly apolitical AllRecipes. com and Cooks.com. McCain's ended up on RecipeZaar. Both campaigns ran ads on the Food Network site. Romney ads were served on Top Secret Recipes.

Why cooking sites? The campaigns could be there for little cost through ad network buys targeted to sites with significant numbers of female visitors. The McCain campaign went after conservatives where they flocked in the hopes of drumming up donations: Right wing news and opinion sites like TownHall.com, National Review, and David Horowitz's FrontPage Magazine. The ads with pro-life and conservative Supreme Court judge nomination themes were intended for such audiences.

And, recognizing the negative reaction Mahmoud Ahmadinejad elicits among some Jews and pro-Israel evangelicals, ads picturing Obama alongside the controversial Iranian President were aimed at religious sites. Evidently, the ads did very well, reaping lots of signups.

The McCain campaign relied far less on efforts to reach niche groups. No staffer was in charge of engaging influential voters on evangelical blogs, social networks or forums, for instance. The campaign also failed to make a concerted online effort to woo the libertarian wing of the Republican Party, which fueled early momentum for Ron Paul and Mitt Romney.

"I didn't see them doing a huge amount of outreach to the libertarian community," said Republican tech consultant Mike Turk. "I think that may have ended up harming them. I think the Web certainly would have been the place to do that."

Hispanics were an important voting bloc who came out heavily for Obama and other Democrats in 2008. The Pew Hispanic Center reported after the election that they voted for the Obama/ Biden ticket by a margin of more than 2-to-1 over McCain/Palin. The Democratic Party and the Obama camp reached out to those voters on the Web.

"¿Estas Registrado Para Votar?" means "Are You Registered to Vote?" and it's what the DNC asked in online ads in the summer of 2008. They appeared to be the first Spanish-language display ads placed in the 2008 election -- and possibly any U.S. presidential election. Mimicking English language DNC ads, they used an Iraq-related message, reminding voters that 4,000 U.S. casualties had resulted from the war, and suggesting "America Is Less Safe."

The Obama camp had its own Web appeal to Spanish speakers. Google searches for "Registrado Para Votar" turned up sponsored links telling users they could register online in just three minutes to vote for Obama.

Two of the groups most targeted by the Obama camp were blacks and young people. The campaign reached black voters through ad buys on BET.com, BlackPlanet.com, and Black America Web. Younger people were targeted through MTV.com and Facebook. Connecting with these audiences via online communities became a cornerstone of the Obama campaign.

"Without re-stating the obvious, we had plans to target the Youth, Women (Wal Mart), and Hispanics going back over a year," wrote McCain internet strategist Eric Frenchman on his blog following the election. "Women in particular we were targeting both with messaging as well as online media for a long time (way BEFORE Hillary dropped out of the race). Even for Hispanics we ran our own in-language search marketing campaigns in Yahoo and Google, but sadly we could never get traction outside of search for these groups."

The McCain, Obama, and Romney camps also used retargeting technology to reach voters with specific appeals based on previous interactions. The way it worked for the Obama campaign, and most likely the others, is a standard practice conducted by countless commercial advertisers and

Web site publishers.

Social networking sites or other Web sites where Obama had a presence could track people who visited Obama-related content (by dropping non-personally identifiable pixels on their computers). Then, through relationships with ad networks, those people could be recognized when visiting other Web sites (basically as a number associated with their computer), and delivered a targeted ad. Or, if someone searched for Obama-related information or issues relevant to his campaign, he might be retargeted on another site.

This technique allowed the campaign to limit ad delivery to people who already appeared to be interested. Plus, they could layer on other forms of targeting such as geographic targeting. A few days before a primary, people living in that state who previously visited the Obama Facebook page or searched Google for information about him might have been served GOTV ads that others didn't see.

This technique was also used on the official campaign sites. For instance, if a would-be supporter went to the donation page but didn't give, the campaign might retarget that person with an e-mail message or Web ad in the hopes of wooing her back.

Retargeting is non-personally identifiable, meaning the data used is anonymous. Still, people aren't always comfortable with the practice of retargeting or other forms of online ad targeting. Indeed, there's one form of targeting that's especially interesting to political advertisers that they tend to keep close to the vest for that very reason.

After the 2000 election, it seemed like everybody in the online politics community was talking about micro-targeting. The Bush/Cheney campaign had employed data mining and segmentation technology to slice and dice voter groups, and what better place to employ such refined sets of data but the Internet?

Voters could be targeted using commercial data – from standard demographics to the type of car someone drives or whether she lives in a one-bedroom apartment or a three-story suburban home. Though it was like pulling teeth to get anyone to speak about the practice, online political insiders revealed that by the 2006 midterm election season commercial data were being merged with voter file data and site publisher registration data, making for super-strength ad targeting databases.

"There's a lot of information being added to a voter registration file," one source familiar with the subject said. He said he'd been involved with recent campaigns that had supplemented voter data with information such as the magazines someone subscribed to in order to target online ads. "It's limitless in terms of what you can do to embellish it with added information," he said.

Political advertiser data and site registration data are merged by a third party, creating a file used by site publishers to target ads to people who were registered on their Web sites. This approach works well when dealing with big Web portals, though certainly social networking sites could also enable this type of ad targeting using profile data. MySpace, for instance, can target ads to small segments of site members using their profile data – New York Mets fans living in New Jersey, or people aged 18 to 34 who list NBC's "The Office" as a favorite TV show, for example (though it's unclear whether the site has done so for political advertisers).

"These are the kinds of things that I think smart people would keep to themselves," one interactive political consultant said, alluding to the privacy concerns associated with tapping information like voter history and party affiliation for targeting ads.

A spokesman for a major Web portal site said the site had done that type of targeting "for years," noting, "We have the ability to take extra data and match it up with our member database…. It's a fairly common process." He stressed the data was secure. "We control the data at all times."

Savvy consumers are accustomed to advertisers combining

information from various sources to better tailor offers to them. However, when advertisers attach data on their shopping habits with info on which party's primaries they've voted in, the dander goes up.

A campaign consultant discussed a 2004 Republican organization that matched voter file data against AOL and Yahoo databases to target ads. The organization provided the voter file information, and the third party data firm ran a match against the registration info and refined the list based on additional criteria such as party affiliation. Then, in the last few weeks before the election, when those particular users showed up on AOL or Yahoo, they may have been served an ad with a GOTV message. The issue-based animated ads dealt with topics like education or national security and were linked to pages allowing users to determine their voting location by entering a street address.

Yet, although such techniques have helped inform campaigns about which groups to target and how, they weren't necessarily effective in previous elections or in 2008. And they weren't always applied this time around when it came to targeting ads or e-mail to tiny tribes of voters online. The McCain campaign dabbled. The Obama campaign did, too, but neither saw micro-targeting as the be-all end-all. The reality is there isn't always enough of a benefit to warrant the cost of using very refined data segmentation to target tiny slivers of voters.

In addition, tailoring ads to appeal to a small audience segment could backfire. Patrick Ruffini, former RNC eCampaign director and partner at Republican online consulting outfit Engage, took a skeptical view of micro-targeting, suggesting it could lead to "danger in over-segmenting the electorate." In his July 2008 post on TechPresident, he explained, "If you're using the technology to divine minute differences between 80 different segments of the electorate and then sending them 80 different messages, you need your head examined.... As brilliant as the Obama/Bush microtargeting model is, both candidates understood the power of central, unifying messages that cut through the clutter. Why is the word most associated with Obama 'change'? Message discipline!"

Although both the McCain and Obama camps used various methods of targeting pockets of voters online – from geographic and demographic targeting to retargeting and simple contextual targeting based on Web site content – none of this was innovative. It's commonplace among commercial advertisers.

# THE SOCIAL EXPERIMENT

"I am officially a member of BlackPlanet.com! Come and check out my page and join my group," declared Obama's "featured profile" promotion on the homepage of the black social network.

Community Connect, publisher of BlackPlanet.com and other ethnic and lifestyle-oriented social networks like the Latino-focused MiGente.com and Glee.com, a network for gays, lesbians "and everyone else," took in over $60,000 in ad revenues from the Obama campaign in 2008.

"They're making sure African-American voters are actively engaged and come out to vote," Community Connect President and CEO Benjamin Sun said.

Obama's campaign didn't just run ads on BlackPlanet, though. After launching profile pages on all of Community Connect's social networking sites in 2007, Obama's Internet team regularly fed new information into them. Updates were often of special relevance to the communities catered to by each network. A video posted to his BlackPlanet profile, for example, featured Obama visiting a barbershop in South Carolina. His Glee.com profile included a post about National Coming Out Day. The MiGente page touted the endorsement of Obama's energy plan by former U.S. Secretary of Energy Federico Pena. Profiles on AsianAve.com, MiGente, and BlackPlanet.com spotlighted education and family issues. Statements on Glee.com highlighted environmental issues. FaithBase.com and AsianAve.com noted Obama's thoughts on faith and politics.

In addition to Obama's main profile, the campaign dedicated individual pages to residents of every state. And keeping with the local approach, many of the ads seen on BlackPlanet were targeted to members living in specific locales. They also bought bulletin-like ads that were served to his Community Connect friends.

While the content updates on his profile and state pages acted as a way to "get people informed and interested in him and believing in him," said Sun, "the advertising gets them to take action." Many of the display ads seen on the social net were the same Obama "Join Us" ads seen across the Web throughout his campaign.

The Obama campaign has "taken a real hands-on engaging [approach], much more so than I've even seen with [other] advertisers," Sun said. "I think his team really gets how to leverage and engage a social networking audience, especially an African-American networking audience."

The Community Connect relationship came about more organically than strategically. Indeed, advertising with the company's niche social networks wasn't necessarily part of the original plans. It all started when the campaign discovered traffic coming to its official site through a profile of musical act Ahmir on BlackPlanet in September 2007. Ahmir was included in BlackPlanet's music section as part of a Vibe Magazine program, and because that month's issue of Vibe featured Obama on the cover, the Ahmir profile linked to BarackObama.com.

"We ended up sending an awful lot traffic to Obama's Web site," Tracey Cooper, director of BlackPlanet, said.

The Obama camp wanted to know how to tap into that audience.

By October, profile pages were up on AsianAve.com, Glee.com, MiGente.com and Christian networking site FaithBase.com. According to Cooper, Obama's director for external organizing had been her point of contact ever since.

Candidates or other advertisers "shouldn't think about setting up profiles on our sites as re-tasking general marketing content," Community Connect vice president of marketing Kay Madati said.

Even before Obama's campaign got in touch with Community Connect, the firm had pitched other presidential primary campaigns, including Clinton's team. "We actually reached out to [Hillary Clinton's] campaign," said Sun, "and the online campaign people just kind of ignored it."

Early in the primary season there appeared to be some interest, however. According to Madati, after the Obama campaign launched profile pages on the publisher's sites, people from the Clinton and Edwards camps inquired about setting up profiles.

Advertisers often cite concern about having their brands associated with inappropriate content on social networking sites. But the Obama camp was worried about just the opposite: inappropriate ads on its profile pages. It wouldn't have looked good, for instance, if ads promoting "Asian Girl Photos" showed up on Obama's AsianAve profile.

Thus, Obama campaign worked with Community Connect to ensure a potentially damaging situation like that didn't occur. The publisher blocked paid ads  on Obama's profile pages, and instead ran ads promoting its own offerings such as BlackPlanet Music or MiGente Music.

Subsets of Obama supporters cropped up on Facebook. There were "Students for Barack Obama," "Latinos for Obama," "Obama Pride," a gay community, and "First Americans for Obama," a group for Native Americans. Similar coalitions were present on Obama's acclaimed networking and organizing site, My.BarackObama.com as well as McCain's social site McCainSpace.

"Obama's legion of followers defied logic," lamented Frenchman on his blog after the election.

The Obama campaign used Facebook to reach users in particular states to organize rallies, attend local events, or help with voter registration. Still, most of the paid Facebook efforts were national in their approach and didn't target niche groups.

The Obama camp spent hundreds of thousands of dollars on Facebook ads. The McCain camp spent next to nothing on the site, though Facebook salespeople pitched them on buying ads.

Near election day, the McCain campaign did finally break down and bought Facebook ads to target college students in one area of the country, urging them to assist with voter registration. "We did some advertising in Facebook, and for a very small micro-target it performed great but didn't scale," Frenchman noted in a blog post after the election.

There was already a close connection between the Obama camp and Facebook in Chris Hughes, Obama's 20-something online organizing coordinator who played a lead role in creating Obama's social site My.BarackObama.com. Hughes is also a Facebook co-founder.

During the election season, reporters and pundits often gushed over Obama's engaging interactive social strategy. Media coverage of anything linking Obama to the Internet inevitably mentioned social networking. Facebook was the poster child.

In June 2008, the Pew Internet & American Life Project reported that 10 percent of Americans used social networking sites "to gather information or become involved" in the primaries.

In September, Pew deemed the Obama campaign "deeply active in the social networking world." Noting Obama's "dominance over McCain," Pew's Project for Excellence in Journalism suggested Obama's "larger social networking base gives the Obama campaign a more sizeable built-in audience of supporters for direct updates and appeals."

But the actual effect of the social networking seemed somewhat nebulous. Sure, the candidate amassed over 3 million Facebook friends compared to McCain's 611,000. But was Obama's Facebook networking really a key factor in voter turnout?

Despite the hype that swirled around social networking and its effects on the election, some online politicos – even Obama supporters and evangelists of digital marketing techniques – questioned their significance.

"Social networking? Despite all of the attention paid to it in (occasionally breathless) media coverage, and the dutiful recording of the candidates' soc net numbers by sites like techPresident, Facebook, MySpace, et al have not proven to be terribly effective tools for campaigns," wrote online communications and advocacy consultant Colin Delany on his e.politics site in the spring of 2008. "Does anyone really think that the fact that Obama has five times as many Facebook friends as Hillary Clinton has turned out to be significant? Demographically interesting and revealing, sure, but actually relevant to how the Democratic primary process has gone so far?"

McCain's Web people clearly wished they could have devoted more resources to social networking. In various post-election blog lamentations, McCain's online ad man Eric Frenchman noted the huge hurdles McCain was up against: George W. Bush's "dismal approval ratings," the economy, the lack of money, not to mention "the greatest use of social networking marketing in the history of the internet in the form of Barack Obama."

He admitted the campaign could have employed social media better to battle attacks. "The only way to have combated that was with a more social networking strategy and better blogger direction," he wrote.

Both the Obama and McCain campaigns regularly added video, news alerts, blog posts, and other content to their Facebook pages. McCain's campaign developed applications for Facebook. They developed their answer to the My.BarackObama.com social networking site, but McCainSpace prompted "boos" from Web pundits who panned it for not being open or social enough.

Throughout the election season, strategists and pundits on the left and right shot down the campaign's social media efforts – or lack thereof. Some thought it seemed like the McCain approach to social networking was more like checking off a box in a long list of "Things to do on the Web" than a wholehearted attempt.

In the end, as far as some McCain people were concerned, the social media interaction failed for the same reasons that plagued the overall campaign: Not enough people and not enough cash. "[A]s much as social networking costs next to nothing when compared with advertising, it still costs money to develop widgets and content," Frenchman wrote in a blog post. "Social networking done correctly needs people to do the outreach."

But a post-election visit to McCain's official Facebook page served as an indication that the McCain camp may not have had its heart in it. As late as January 2009, Facebook.com/JohnMcCain still listed the Arizona senator as "Currently Running For Office: President."

How many people and how much money would it have taken to bring the page up to date? It's a rhetorical question, but the answer is "one person and no money."

And, though members were still submitting videos and writing blog posts on McCainSpace a month after the election, there was little if any recognition that the election had occurred. Surely McCain or Palin will want to reach out to those Facebook and McCainSpace members for support in future initiatives. Wouldn't it make sense to continue cultivating those relationships even when it's not politically expedient?

Obama's Facebook page, meanwhile, greeted visitors with a bright "Thank You" image after the election and updated videos including one featuring his election night speech. And, in an effort to maintain the momentum achieved through the social tools it had provided, the campaign swiftly shifted toward harnessing its online communities to support him in his transition to president.

Observers of Obama's Facebook interaction said it was light years ahead of what McCain and earlier primary campaigns did on the site. The Obama team updated appearance schedules for Obama, Biden and Michelle Obama. Staffers used the social network as a place to organize, respond to comments, and get people to events rather than simply establish a page for supporters to write messages on a virtual wall.

Another component of Obama's Facebook strategy: advertising. The "rah-rah Facebook" media coverage didn't mention much about that part, but it may have fueled the Obama camp's success on the site. As with many commercial campaigns on social sites, paid ads may have jumpstarted the Obama Facebook phenomenon.

The campaign served ads to Democrats, liberals, and independents aged 18 and over in key states throughout 2008. Some ads allowed users to watch video or post comments. Some ads were served to anyone in key states who was eligible to vote. Most were used to promote local events, organize voters, and push voter registration or early voting.

At least half of Obama's Facebook ads were purchased by the national campaign, while some were placed by local campaign operations. Many of those promoted local campaign events and were simple ads made with the site's ad creation tool.

"They thought about how ads get integrated into driving behavior in a more immediate way," said Facebook vice president of media sales, Mike Murphy.

When it came to the advertising, Facebook worked directly with two or three campaign staffers, including Hughes, on a regular basis. Not surprising, the My.BarackObama.com site eventually enabled Facebook Connect, a platform that lets users sign in on other Web sites with their Facebook account information, to interact on those sites with their Facebook pals.

"What they figured out really early was it's creating a connection with the consumer, and that creates influence within their circle," said Facebook's public policy lead, Chris Kelly.

MoveOn also had its own significant Facebook ad campaign supporting Obama throughout the election.

Practically everyone selling any form or online advertising pitched McCain's Web people. Facebook's sales team did, too, suggesting that advertising with the social network would help McCain reach new audiences and energize existing supporters.

They were up against some big barriers. Although McCain's online ad man Frenchman wrote on his blog that social sites are "critical for involving supporters and pushing CRM [Customer/Constituent Relationship Management] messages," he freely admitted he's "not a believer in using social networking sites for paid online advertising." He said it's a waste.

It's also possible the McCain people didn't want to buy ads on a site that was co-founded by a guy who was playing a key role in Obama's online strategy.

# VIDEO, MOBILE, AND EMERGING MEDIA

In 2004, YouTube did not exist.

Let that sink in for a moment.

Now consider this. Then, in the somewhat insular world of digital politics, it seemed as though when the topic of viral video came up, all anyone talked about was JibJab – the company behind the animated video featuring photo collage-like images of George W. Bush and John Kerry singing a parody of a Woody Guthrie tune.

The "This Land" video would change politics as we knew it, they said. When Web pundits talked about the JibJab video, they lumped it in with seemingly unrelated things like the torture photos from Abu Ghraib – only because a lot of people had seen both as a result of easy Internet dissemination.

The animated Bush and Kerry traded barbs, with Bush calling Kerry a "liberal sissy" and "pinko commie." Bush was a "right wing nut job" and "dumb as a doorknob." Both declared, "This

In 2004, people had watched "This Land" over 65 million times, passing it around to one another. And it had something to do with politics…sort of. Imagine if a real political campaign could harness that sort of (inexpensive) people power! The techno-politicos loved this.

"[W]e're clearly in a new environment for political media," wrote Micah Sifry, co-founder and editor of Personal Democracy Forum and TechPresident, in an October 2004 blog post on the PDF site, which is dedicated to studying the connection of politics and technology. "It sure seems like we are seeing the emergence of an alternative ad-hoc distribution system, one that makes all the old capital-intensive ways of moving a message seem like a waste of money."

It's easy to mock the notion that the JibJab video changed politics. Of course, it didn't. A confluence of factors enabled the coming impact of online video on the political sphere: wide adoption of high-speed Internet services, easy publishing tools, and social media platforms to name a few.

By 2007, online political video no longer meant silly animations. Politicians had been caught on camera saying things that had cost them elections after enough people had watched it on YouTube (and once the mainstream press paid attention). Former Virginia Sen. George Allen's "macaca moment" is a prime example. Allen was caught on video during an event using the slur to refer to an opponent's campaign operative of Southeast Asian decent.

Before that, Swift Boat Veterans for Truth, an advocacy group, uploaded an ad to the Web that had a huge effect on Kerry's failed presidential campaign. The ad portrayed the Vietnam Vet as a traitor against his country and military for protesting the War when he returned from service.

By 2007, when the primary campaigns started to heat up, YouTube was a household brand, and online political video had substance. It had Obama Girl, and that talking snowman from the YouTube presidential debate.

All right, so there was still a lot of video masquerading as politically relevant that probably wasn't. But there was a significant amount of material that was relevant. Political campaigns featured exclusive Web-only video on their sites, created channels on YouTube, and embedded video clips in their Web ads.

The McCain campaign recognized the value of Web video so well that his general counsel publicly asked YouTube to stop removing some of McCain's videos. YouTube should "commit to a full legal review of all takedown notices on videos posted from accounts controlled by (at least) political candidates and campaigns," John McCain for President's attorney, Trevor Potter, wrote in October 2008 to YouTube CEO Chad Hurley and the attorneys for YouTube and Google. He also sent a copy to Barack Obama's campaign.

Potter complained that several of McCain's campaign videos had been removed "numerous times" unnecessarily as a result of questionable copyright infringement claims. Typically in such cases, a video in question included footage from a television news outlet. YouTube's answer, in so many words was "tough luck." The company responded, suggesting the McCain campaign use legal methods of counteracting video removal and copyright infringement claims.

Both the Obama and McCain campaigns were subject to YouTube video cleansing. In September, a McCain video referencing a controversial Obama comment was removed from the site. The video featured Obama questioning McCain's claim that he would change Washington: "You can put lipstick on a pig, but it's still a pig," he said. The comment recalled a one-liner told by McCain running mate Sarah Palin, a self-proclaimed hockey mom, during her speech at the Republican National Convention a few days before: "They say the difference between a hockey mom and a pitbull: lipstick." Republicans called for Obama to apologize for what they considered a smear against Palin.

The McCain video also included footage of "CBS Evening News" anchor Katie Couric stating, "One of the great lessons of that campaign is the continued and accepted role of sexism in American life." Couric had actually been alluding to Clinton's campaign. CBS requested removal of the Web video, and YouTube complied.

The following month an Obama video disappeared from

YouTube. It promoted voter registrations, and spliced together clips of NBC anchors to make it seem as though they had declared McCain the winner of the presidential election. The Obama camp named the video "Bad News." NBC requested a takedown, granted by YouTube.

"We have seen a lot of blogs and TV networks peeved at the candidates using clips or their content inside their political ads, especially attack ads," said Rajeev Kadam, CEO of Divinity Metrics, a firm that measures Web video consumption. "This election especially, content owners [referencing] attack ads are being very vocal because they view that type of content as damaging to their brand and impartiality. For YouTube, it's a safer bet to just take them down instead of inviting a lawsuit."

According to data from Divinity Metrics, about 40 videos placed by the McCain campaign had been removed, while about 10 from the Obama camp were no longer available on the video site.

"YouTube has become a critical distribution arm. Any time that's endangered – whether you're the McCain campaign or a guy in your garage – it becomes an issue for you," said Robert Greenwald. The progressive political filmmaker and founder of Brave New Films, an organization that had been using video placed on YouTube to fight McCain's campaign and promote progressive political ideas, had experienced his own run-ins with YouTube takedowns.

The YouTube-McCain dustup indicates how important Web video is to politicians and why, suggested Tod Sacerdoti , CEO of Brightroll, a video ad network. While political campaigns need to "very quickly regurgitate news or other copyrighted content in the video ecosystem," there aren't many other types of advertisers who have that same immediate requirement. "There's a daily media cycle in politics that doesn't impact other industries in the same way. There's a lot of really important information that means nothing tomorrow."

YouTube also acted as an incubator for the campaigns, said Sacerdoti. "It seemed like a great testing ground for ideas…. You can either take that creative and use it on television, or further explore the content."

Web video wouldn't matter at all if people didn't watch it. Between the 2004 and 2008 elections, it went from being an afterthought to a must. That was driven by a significant increase in online video viewing.

"Video is now a central part of the online experience for people in a way it wasn't in 2004," said Pew Internet & American Life Project Director Lee Rainie. A report from the research outfit showed that 35 percent of survey respondents watched online political videos – nearly triple the number who did four years before.

Web video is synonymous with YouTube, and political campaigns know that. The McCain and Obama camps both made sure they had a prominent presence on the video site. But Obama got a lot more action. Videos uploaded by his campaign attracted nearly double the amount of views on peak viewing days, according to Divinity Metrics. In early and late October 2008  videos on Obama's official YouTube channel were viewed around 1.5 million times in a day.

But the McCain camp never managed to spur that kind of interest. The most views his YouTube channel attracted was around 800,000 a day in July – accounting for all the campaign's YouTube videos available at the time. By the time the election was closing in, as Obama's campaign was grabbing over a million views on some days, McCain was attracting only about 200,000.

And the Obama team offered a lot more to choose from. Compared to 376 videos uploaded to YouTube by the McCain camp, the Obama people put up over 1,980, according to Divinity. And Obama fueled far more user-generated videos – those not associated officially with the campaign – than did McCain. The video research firm found over 104,000 videos related to Obama across the Web during the election season; about 64,000 were related to his opponent.

"McCain, sadly, was not big on video," said Divinity Metrics's Kadam. "McCain did create spikes, though, in viewership because of the heated campaign."

The candidates' official site video views painted a different picture, at least according to Nielsen Online. In September 2008, the number of video streams on JohnMcCain.com hit 3.2 million while the official Obama site served up around 2 million streams that month. Both, however, had around the same number of individual video viewers (1.3 for McCain and 1.1 for Obama).

Both campaigns clearly cared about online video and dedicated resources to it. While political campaigns employ most digital marketing tactics for list building and fundraising, video is different. Perhaps its most significant purpose – on YouTube and in ads – is persuasion. There's nothing like the moving image coupled with sound to captivate an audience, especially when that audience chooses to watch as opposed to being a captive audience.

Not only do television ads interrupt the viewer, they cost a lot doing it. Campaigns can run the same ads on the Web, in addition to all sorts of other video content, for far less.

That was especially beneficial for the cash-strapped McCain camp. "We used YouTube from the very beginning," wrote McCain online ad man Eric Frenchman on his PardonMyFrench blog after the election. "When the campaign imploded during the primary season we had to use YouTube to push out video ads. Web video was a key strategy for us especially before we won New Hampshire."

However, he didn't necessarily buy the notion that every political campaign could foster a viral video phenomenon. "While I believe there were quite a number of people that supported Senator McCain that would spontaneously create videos, Senator

Obama as well as Congressman Ron Paul had a much larger pool of people that would create content," Frenchman wrote, suggesting positive videos uploaded by McCain supporters were few and far between. "Heck, even our best professional fan video - Raisin' McCain by John Rich only generated 152,000 views." The video was a sleek production featuring the upbeat country artist crooning about how the former Navy pilot "got shutdown in a Vietnam town, fightin' for the red, white, and blue."

"We loaded up YouTube videos," Frenchman said after the election. "Our constituents didn't send stuff out virally....The people that were attracted to us weren't the type that would spontaneously make a video."

All in all, the campaigns didn't do a lot when it came to paid video advertising. But they did use some video ads during the primaries and beyond. Mitt Romney's campaign ran innovative video overlay ads in October 2007, repurposing TV spots that were also on air in Iowa. Not only did they aim to persuade, they allowed the viewer to click-through to the "Join Team Mitt" registration page on MittRomney.com.

"Mitt says there's no work more important than what goes on inside the four walls of the American home, and that's the way it was in our home," said Romney's wife in the ad.

The campaign used ScanScout's video platform to make sure ads were placed alongside socially-conservative and family related video content. The overlay ad appeared below the video content. When users clicked to view the ads, the content video paused.

The Romney campaign also used expandable video-enabled ads comparing the former Massachusetts governor's pro-life and pro-traditional marriage stances with those of Republican Mike Huckabee.

During the primaries and in spurts during the general election season, McCain's "Courageous Service" video showed up in video-enabled banners.

The Obama camp made a big push with video in their eye-catching local news site ads before the Texas and Ohio primaries. The ads expanded to reveal a variety of TV spots in the combined persuasion/GOTV effort. To reinforce those ads – and other display ads targeted to voters in important primary states like North Carolina, Indiana, and Pennsylvania – the campaign used in-stream video advertising. Those streaming ads were TV spots shown before or during video clips.

Why buy in-stream video ads? "On some level there was so much money that you couldn't buy any more TV," said one source who worked on the video ad buys during the primaries. The campaign also appreciated the fact that the Web could extend the TV message to a different audience.

Some of Obama's early voting ads also featured video in the final weeks of the election. Still, in comparison to their practically free video placements on YouTube and other free video sites, the presidential campaigns used paid video advertising sparingly.

In addition to its positive association with social media and online organizing prowess, the Obama campaign became known as the tech savvy foil to McCain's computer cluelessness. The perception was McCain was the fuddy-duddy who didn't get it, while the Obama camp was all about emerging media, embracing mobile messaging as a means of reaching young voters. He even ran ads in online games! The press ate it up.

The Obama camp developed a WAP site and created an iPhone application. The mainstream news media hyped their use of text messaging to announce the choice of Sen. Joe Biden as Obama's running mate. The campaign pushed voter registration and early voting through geographically targeted mobile text alerts.

As the election neared, they used novel ad formats to push early voting. Users of online music service Pandora in battleground states were greeted with an Obama-themed interface before the election. Banner ads targeted younger people in early voting states through Boost Mobile's network. Users could opt-in to learn more about where to vote in their area.

"They really leveraged the medium as a whole across all different touch-points," suggested Paran Johar, chief marketing officer of mobile ad network and search firm JumpTap. "I think it's the channel that's the difference," he said after the election. "It reached a much different audience than McCain."

To some campaign observers, the McCain people didn't seem to get the Web much less mobile. Didn't they want to connect to younger voters? Didn't they want to prove that McCain wasn't the technical ignoramus people were making him out to be?

Yet people in the McCain camp wanted just that and were willing to do something splashy with mobile months before Obama's VP text announcement made headlines. The folks holding the purse-strings said "no," declaring a big mobile effort a big waste of time.

The RNC did send out last-minute get-out-the-vote text messages in English and Spanish via a mobile ad network on election day, though.

The Obama campaign also placed its early voting messages in unique places like free directory information calls. People in Iowa, Ohio, Indiana, Montana, Wisconsin, North Carolina, New Mexico, Colorado, or Florida who dialed 1-800-Free-411 (often using their mobile phones) heard Obama audio ads before getting requested contact information for nearby Thai restaurants or dry cleaners. The ads were delivered through Jingle Networks, operator of the free directory service.

Obama's camp even ran ads in online games in October. The campaign spent around $90,000 with Microsoft-owned in-game ad network Massive to run Obama's Vote for Change message on virtual billboards in EA games like high-speed driving diversion "Burnout Paradise." The ads were targeted to gamers in 10 battleground states, according to a Washington newspaper, The Hill.

"Candidates are clearly waking up to the 21st century and realizing that voters are no longer glued to the television," Bassik said. "To reach voters, you have to go where they are. And in a race this close, I wouldn't be surprised to see political ads on the back of bathroom stalls. No stone should be left unturned."

Still, it's questionable whether the campaign really believed the ads would work, or whether they bought them simply for their sheer novelty and potential to grab media attention. Clearly, as indicated in Ryan Lizza's post-election New Yorker article on the Obama campaign strategy, there was a little bit of, "Hey, why the hell not?" involved in that media buying decision.

"I mean, dude… when you're buying commercials in video games, you truly are being well funded," quipped Obama campaign chief of staff Jim Messina in the article.

While the Obama camp got lots of praise for being innovative, forward-thinking, and downright hip for its in-game ad tactic, the idea might not have originated with them. In fact, EA Games and Jingle Networks pitched the McCain campaign too.

# MEASURING SUCCESS

As the McCain campaign rubbed pennies together, the Obama campaign was rolling in a field of greenbacks. Did the Obama people even have to prove the value of their digital ad spending? From the looks of things they were running ads everywhere online. Were they even held to any standards?

Some worried. Web evangelists who had dedicated their careers to showing political campaigns the online light wondered: If the most prominent, most talked-about digital political campaign in history didn't have the numbers to back it up, what would the naysayers think? They could easily point to the Obama campaign as one that did so much on the Web simply because they could afford to do anything and everything. Who says the Web ads or the text messaging really worked?

Measurement is a double-edged sword for digital marketers. Unlike any other medium – television, direct mail, print, radio, lawn signs – spending on digital media can be measured relatively precisely. There's no telling how many people actually watched a television spot, much less paid attention to it.

Not so with Web ads. Because they're all digital, a user's interactions can be tracked based on whether or not he clicked or where he clicked within an ad. Advertisers can track the number of people who clicked an ad, how many submitted their e-mail address or donated on the campaign site, or how long they viewed a video placed in an ad unit.

The amount of money spent on a particular effort – say a voter registration search ad campaign targeted to Pennsylvanians – can be measured against the number of actual voter registration forms filled out online. A dollar amount can be attached to each goal. If each voter registration is worth $3 to a campaign, and it cost them $0.75 to run the 1,000 impressions of the ad that drove five people to click through and register, the return on investment is positive. Of course, it's even easier to measure the value of a fundraising effort. The ROI for an individual ad is the donation amount minus the ad cost. The Web team would look at the results of an ad campaign in aggregate to determine its overall value.

The McCain Web team was held to rigid standards. Because money was so tight, they had to prove the value of their ad spending day in and day out – and the statistics were readily available. Again, the measurability of online advertising is a blessing and a curse. Because value can be proved, it must be proved – especially when every cent spent is so closely monitored. Even years after running particular online ad campaigns, commercial advertisers don't like to share specific results for fear of the competition exploiting them. For the same reason, neither the Obama nor the McCain campaign will lay their cards on the table for inspection. But all signs point to a very accountable online campaign effort by the Obama team. Talks with media firms that worked with the Obama team as well as even closer sources say they were extremely ROI-focused.

"They knew by the hour how much money their ads were making," said a media exec who worked closely with the Obama digital ad staff. "There were no slouches on the Obama team," he added. In fact, his observations of their data-driven decision-making and campaign measurement led the executive to call one top Obama digital ad staffer a "quant."

The Obama campaign paid $22,000 to Dynamic Logic, a research firm that measures things like brand impact of digital advertising and cross-media ad effectiveness.

The Obama Web team had a specific goal set for every individual online effort – from geo-targeted Facebook ads to nationally aimed search ads. A main reason they invested in the Web in the first place, said one source close to the campaign, was because they could prove its worth. They wouldn't have done it if it didn't work.

Indeed, when something didn't work, it was cut. When something did, it might have gotten a bigger chunk of the budget the next month.

Both the McCain and Obama campaigns used standard metrics to measure their Web ads. Because most of their ad campaigns were focused on direct response goals (signups, donations, voter registrations), they gauged success accordingly based on cost per click, cost per acquisition, or cost per action. How much did it cost on average for someone to click-through on an ad or submit contact information?

The primary candidates did it, too. Romney for President's e-strategy director Mindy Finn said  the campaign measured ad success by the number of volunteer signups it gathered or the value of contributions it collected as a result of click through. The Romney team devised a formula based on how many potential Iowa caucus voters, for instance, were reached per dollar spent.

Like any savvy commercial marketer, the McCain and Obama campaigns tested and optimized their ad tactics. They measured the response to changes in search ads or the "ask" in a display ad. Obama's ads varied to such a degree that sometimes it was difficult to notice the differences. In testing multiple iterations of an ad in order to determine which ad copy had the best results, "Visit the official campaign website" became "Visit the official Barack Obama website." Each variation was compared to the others to determine which got the most people to click through or donate.

The campaigns also used tools to test and optimize the content on landing pages, the Web pages people were taken to after clicking an ad.

Significantly, the Obama campaign evaluated efforts across media platforms. While there's no standard equation for measuring the value of a television campaign against the value of a Web ad campaign or a debate night house party, the Obama campaign tried to compare them by applying a cost-per-acquisition metric to all media. For instance, it might have measured a door-to-door canvassing campaign against a search ad campaign by determining the average cost of each voter registered through each mode of acquiring that registration.

Commercial marketers continue to grapple with digital ad measurement, still arguing over the importance or validity of the most basic metrics, like ad click throughs. As new digital platforms and ad formats proliferate, ad measurement becomes even more tricky. Commercial marketers and Web site publishers are a long way from agreeing on standards for Web ad measurement. We can expect the same for political advertisers.

# CONCLUSION

2008 was not THE Internet election.

But it's worth pondering whether Barack Obama could have won the Democratic nomination and the election without it. What really fueled the momentum behind the candidate? It was the candidate, himself, of course. And people working on Obama's Web campaign said what they were doing wouldn't necessarily have worked for another candidate. All the online organizing tools and savvy marketing in the world can't do much if the product doesn't get people fired up.

The field organizing operation was said to be a huge factor. Online advertising, social networking, organizing tools, and e-mail helped mobilize supporters. But campaign insiders recognized the in-person interaction – the feet on the street – played a huge role in Obama's campaign success.

And what of all that talk of a new legion of small donors, who were willing to get involved AND donate? The reality may not have lived up to the hype.

In February, the Obama camp reported that 1 million donors had given to his campaign. In August the tally came to 2 million donors "owning a piece of this campaign." Pundits heralded the new era of people-powered politics. No longer would corporate donors and lobbyists rule in Washington, some believed. The

Web and the Obama camp's ability to harness it as an engine for rallying everyday Americans would change everything, and the small donor phenomenon was a first step.

A few weeks after the election, The Washington Post reported that 3 million people donated to the Obama campaign 6.5 million times, and 6 million of those donations were less than $100. Most of the $600 million the Obama campaign raised during the election season came through the Web, according to the article.

Not long after the Post story came out, a non-partisan George Washington University-affiliated non-profit, the Campaign Finance Institute, tempered the small donor-driven excitement. It turned out around 25 percent of Obama's funds came from "donors whose total contributions aggregated to $200 or less," the group noted in a November 24 press release – around the same amount as Bush/Cheney '04. So even though about half of the individual donations were under $200, many people donated multiple times, CFI found by analyzing Obama's FEC reports.

Twenty-one percent of McCain's donations were less than $200. In 2004, Dean did better by people-power standards, with 38 percent coming from small donors, according to CFI.

"After a more thorough analysis of data from the Federal Election Commission (FEC), it has become clear that repeaters and large donors were even more important for Obama than we or other analysts had fully appreciated," stated the organization.

So, the small donor effect may not have been quite as forceful as some assumed. However, the Web's use as a fundraising vehicle and the use of online advertising and e-mail to facilitate fundraising should no longer be in question.

But it's hard not to keep going back to the money. The Web has been considered a great place to collect cash but rarely the place to spend it.

"If you think of what [the Obama campaign] could have done if they trimmed 1 percent off their TV buy… You haven't begun to see what they could have done had the Internet been a slightly larger percentage of the [budget]," Republican consultant Mike Turk said after the election.

The same goes for McCain, said Turk. "Going from 1 percent to 2 percent [for example] could have made a huge difference."

However, Turk thinks the campaigns of tomorrow have plenty to learn from the '08 campaigns' digital strategies. "What is interesting about both campaigns in terms of what it says to future campaigns is…there are ways to use these things effectively regardless of your budget," he said.

Turk is part of a group of Republican Web evangelists who aim to directly apply lessons learned about the importance of integrated digital strategy to ready their party for 2012.

Rather than waste time lamenting, Rebuild the Party is a newly formed coalition of tech savvy Republicans with a focus on using the Web to "start building the future of our party now." The group's mission statement makes it clear: "Barack Obama and the Democrats' ability to build their entire fundraising, GOTV, and communications machine from the Internet is the #1 existential challenge to our existing party model."

They call the Internet their top priority in the next four years, suggesting that an anti-Washington message will help energize the party base, creating a need for a new set of online organizing tools. The group believes that "online organizing is by far the most efficient way to transform our party structures to be able to compete against what is likely to be a $1 billion Obama re-election campaign in 2012."

If their recommendations are implemented, we can expect more Republican campaign money to flow toward the Web. However, we shouldn't necessarily expect much change when it comes to the goals of that spending. For Rebuild the Party, it's still about generating signups and donations. Part of the Internet-centric mission is to "Recruit 5 million new Republican online activists." To do that, the group wants to integrate "e-mail signups into everything we do at the grassroots level." They even want individual Republican candidate campaigns to be held to standards in terms of list-building and fundraising.

They also recognize the assistance Democrats have received through the altruistic open-source technology development movement. Taking advantage of the ability to create new applications for existing open-source platforms, tech developers got together to donate their time and energy to building an iPhone application for the Obama campaign. The Rebuild people hope to draft their own tech army for Republicans, a "corps of outside technology volunteers who compete to write applications that actually improve party operations."

Though some of McCain's Web team might see the new group as an indictment on their digital strategy, Rebuild the Party can certainly be considered much more than that – a collective of people with digital smarts who care about the future of their party and want to make it better by pushing it into the 21st century.

The emergence of the group symbolizes the realization among some Republicans that the Obama campaign's ability to harness the Web played a key role in his win. They clearly believe the Internet to be an undeniably powerful force that must be understood and provided resources if their party is to remain relevant. If Republican Party leaders embrace these concepts, and both major parties compete head-on for digital tech dominance, 2012 could bring us closer to the true "Internet election."

Other Republicans have begun talking about the need to work toward a real, integrated use of the Web, said Campaign Grid's Jeff Dittus. "All roads are pointing in that direction…those discussions are beginning to occur," he said after the election.

Can it work? "I think it's certainly a challenge," said Turk. "Do I think it's an insurmountable challenge? Absolutely not." Turk believes Republicans will begin to use the Internet to build themselves back up in the same way they did with talk radio in the past. "Now that they're out of power, the Republicans will flock to the Internet because it's the most interactive form of media there is."

But, he added, the party needs to create the infrastructure to support that. That means the party establishment will have "to stop thinking of the Internet as this place where evil dwells."

As for the Democrats, they're not looking back. The My.BarackObama.com organizing powerhouse remains active and is expected to stay that way. President-Elect Obama's Change. gov transition Web site allowed people to submit their personal "stories" and "ideas" for helping to "change the future of the country" in text or video. The Obama transition team appeared to understand the need to keep in continual e-mail contact with their huge list of supporters.

Obama's campaign manager, David Plouffe, sent an e-mail to supporters a month after the election asking them to "join your friends and neighbors – sign up to host or attend a Change is Coming house meeting near you." He wrote, "Your ideas and feedback will be collected and used to guide this movement in the months and years ahead."

The trappings of a more open, community-influenced government were evident in the president-elect's online presence. Whether the Obama administration will apply the grassroots-up principles his Web efforts were founded on to governing remains to be seen.

The Obama campaign's e-mail list, estimated at 13 million addresses, has been used by Organizing for America, the Democratic National Committee project established in January to serve as the post-campaign extension of the Obama marketing machine. There's no precedent for a presidential administration directly interacting with supporters using an enormous campaign database, at least in a robust manner. No matter under what auspices, the Obama network of supporters and the data associated with it will not be allowed to wither on the vine. Democrats will nurture – and exploit – it, in the hopes of it growing into a reliable fundraising and organization system for all Democrats. The midterm elections in 2010 will be the first big test.

If the Rebuild Republicans manage to accomplish their mission of convincing the party elite to get serious about digital media, the Democrats cannot rest on their '08 Web campaign laurels if they expect to maintain their majority in Congress for long, much less grow it.

The analysis of Campaign '08 has just begun. Politicos will use it as a guide to Web campaigning for years to come, but there's no telling what technologies and interactive tools will emerge as key the next time around. All students of this year's groundbreaking election must consider the rapid pace at which digital media evolve when tempted to use 2008 as a template for the future.

# AFTERWORD

You are not running for president. Your organization does not define success by having millions of people across the country vote for it. Can you learn anything from the recent elections that will improve the effectiveness of your digital communication efforts?

I think the answer is, "Yes!"

First and foremost, the vast number of people who used digital media to engage with the candidates and the media that covered them should erase any lingering notion that digital techniques don't count. If your colleagues or your superiors don't yet get it, just pull out a few of the statistics from Kate's text. If they still don't get it, you may just want to move on to an organization that does get it. Seriously.

The big lesson about digital media from the campaign: Just do it. Beyond that, however, the campaigns also offer several specific guideposts for success.

**Cultivate Your Fans**

Members of "Generation Obama" exhibit a willingness to communicate with large numbers of people about things that matter to them. And the social nature of digital technology makes it easy for people to share across geographic and established community boundaries. The Obama campaign asked for and motivated this communication all the way through Election Day.

General marketers need to emulate this drive to get their own economic engines humming again. They need to ask their fans and followers to spread positive messages about them – and inspire them to do it. Direct marketing only gets you so far. The validation of real people and the positive reputation created by their digital communications distinguishes winners from losers.

### Integrate with Real Events

Online activities can enhance the impact of an offline event. They can shape expectations and the experience itself – before, during and after.

General marketers can learn a great deal from how the presidential campaigns, and the news media and bloggers that covered them, behaved before, during and after the debates to shape voters' perceptions of the debates themselves.

The outcome of the election was not determined online. Nor was it determined by television advertisements. It was fashioned by real events and the impressions those events left regarding the candidates' ability to lead.

General marketers need to make sure that their digital communications efforts constantly reflect what is happening to them and their different audiences in the real world.

### Bind Real People Together

When the campaign was drawing to a close, the "invisible Web" became most important. What is the "invisible Web"? It is, quite simply, the hard-working stuff you don't see that gets results – the emails, text messages, robocalls and database-generated call sheets. These back-room techniques generate heat and power – just not a lot of flash.

And like invisible light, we can only see the results of the invisible Web, not the activities themselves. For instance, a Washington Post poll found that more than half of the likely voters in Virginia had been contacted in person, on the phone, or by email or text message about voting for Sen. Barack Obama.

I live in Virginia, a battleground state, in a bipartisan household, and I can attest to the number of contacts facilitated by digital means. I received an interactive, voice-recognition robocall from Sen. John McCain's campaign asking if I knew about Obama's relationship with Bill Ayers. And I received phone calls from MoveOn.org volunteers in New Mexico and Connecticut asking me to volunteer.

"The media pays attention to the campaigns' closing arguments," says Melissa Boasberg, a leader of the online effort for Sen. John Kerry's 2004 presidential campaign. "At the end of the campaign online, there are no more arguments. There is only a focus on action."

And that action is to get people to the polls.

In this election cycle, digital tools were the force behind the phone calls and the door-to-door canvases needed to persuade the undecided and drive people to the polls. The digital is driving, reminding, and offering incentives to real people to directly contact others to get them to act.

**Younger People Persuade Older People**

To paraphrase Chris Matthews, the host of MSNC's Hard Ball, this election was about a great generational divide. Mr. Matthews said in a speech that McCain supporters were voting like their grandparents who could not imagine the world we are confronting and Obama supporters were voting like their grandchildren ready to confront a new age.

For general marketers, this is an important insight. If you are trying to provide a product or a service to a more mature audience, you may need to focus some of your efforts on their younger relatives to get the word out.

The point is not whether this inter-generational communication is occurring digitally. (It is.) The point is that the dialogue is highly influential. And most likely, the traditional marketer can best influence this dialogue through digital techniques.

**Serve, Don't Just Market**

During times of transition, the digital world requires marketers to be interactive and transparent. That said, the degree to which they do so may limit their ability to be leaders and innovators. All marketers should watch how Obama makes the transition from candidate to President for guidance on what works and what does not.

It seems to me that in the digital media environment, there are two boundary lines that are now governing the communications playing field: Interaction and transparency. The question for communicators is how transparent and interactive to be while the substance of an organization – its brand meaning – is being formed or fundamentally changed.

According to Robert Rasmussen, an executive creative director at R/GA, the job of marketers is now to create interaction between brands and customers. When organizations have worked hard to develop a dialogue with their different constituencies, what should be done when there is no "time out" during a period of transition? How can an organization even have the time to develop a point of view or a road map?

In this media environment, organizations and brands no longer have the luxury of thoroughly pre-testing messages and decisions before they are communicated. The demand for interaction becomes non-stop.

So, even though you are not running for president, and your organization is not out trolling for millions of votes, it is trying to reach an audience and it is trying to get that audience to take some action. The successes and failures of the presidential campaigns can be powerful tools for helping you improve your organization's marketing and communication efforts.

Dan Solomon
CEO Virilion